THE SOUTHWARK MYSTERIES

First published by Oberon Books in 1999 Oberon Books Ltd
521 Caledonian Rd, London N7 9RH
Tel: 020 7607 3637 Fax: 020 7607 3629
e-mail: info@oberon.books.com
www.oberonbooks.com

Revised edition in 2011.

Item,
that the women of the common brothel
shall be seen every day for what they be,
and a woman that liveth by her body
shall have free licence and liberty
to come and to go at all times,
without any interruption of the Stewholder.

From "The Ordinances touching the Government of the
Stewholders in Southwark under the direction of the Bishop of
Winchester instituted in the Time of Henry the Second, 1161 AD."

A Common Whore

John Constable

THE SOUTHWARK MYSTERIES

OBERON BOOKS
LONDON
WWW.OBERONBOOKS.COM

Contents

Preface

The *Southwark Mysteries* began on the night of 23rd November 1996, when I wrote the first of *The Vision Books* inspired by The Goose, the spirit of a prostitute from Southwark's ancient Liberty of the Clink, licensed by a Bishop yet buried in the unconsecrated Crossbones Graveyard. In these apocalyptic verses, The Goose initiates my trickster familiar John Crow into a secret history - a vision of the Spirit in the flesh, the Sacred in the profane, Eternity in time.

This vision inspires and informs *The Mystery Plays,* a contemporary "Southwark Cycle" rooted in the medieval mysteries, retelling sacred stories in the earthy language and context of our own time and place. The third part of the work is a *Glossolalia* of local history and esoteric lore to be read in conjunction with the poems and plays.

The Southwark Mysteries was first performed in Shakespeare's Globe and Southwark Cathedral, on Easter Sunday, 23rd April 2000. Local MP Simon Hughes called it "the jewel in the crown" of Southwark's millennium celebrations and proposed that it be staged every decade. A new production was presented in Southwark Cathedral in 2010.

In the decade between these epic productions, SOUTHWARK MYSTERIES presented workshops, guided walks and site-specific performances inspired by the work. Selected texts from *The Vision Books* featured in *The Anatomy Class* at The Old Operating Theatre, *The Goose At Liberty* in Southwark Playhouse, and *The Halloween of Crossbones*, a ritual drama conducted annually 1998-2010. The Halloween performance culminated in a candle-lit procession to the gates of Crossbones Graveyard; the red iron gates of the desolate works-site were decorated with ribbons, flowers, feathers, keys, mirrors, jewellery, mementoes and totems, creating a shrine to "the outcast dead".

The Southwark Mysteries reclaimed the lost history of Crossbones, re-envisioning the   forgotten, derelict wasteland as sacred ground, a portal between worlds, a garden of healing and transformation. The gates in Redcross Way have become a place of pilgrimage and Crossbones Graveyard is now recognised as a unique heritage site. Vigils are held at 7pm on the 23rd of every month - to remember the outcast, to renew the shrine and to work towards the creation of a public garden of remembrance on the site of the old burial ground. A wild "Invisible Garden" already grows there.

***

This new edition is dedicated to the Very Reverend Colin Slee, late Dean of Southwark Cathedral. Colin was a powerful advocate for *The Southwark Mysteries* and took an active interest in the work, striving to firm-up its theological foundations. No stranger to controversy, he robustly defended the Easter Sunday 2000 performance in the Cathedral, provoking a *Sunday Telegraph* headline: "Dean rejects critics of Southwark's 'swearing Jesus' Mystery Play". The Dean and Chapter withstood the storm, invited us back and were generous hosts to the 2010 production.

The entire work, and specifically the productions, could got not have been realised without the help and unwavering support of my partner, Katharine Nicholls. I would like to add my thanks to my literary agent Nicki Stoddart and publisher James Hogan, to SOUTHWARK MYSTERIES patrons Mark Rylance and Simon Hughes MP, and to all who supported the productions or worked to manifest the vision at Crossbones. To name but a few:

Beccy Allen, Irene Anderson-King, Katherine Angel, Anna Arthur, Steve Ash, Jimmy Cauty, Dan Clarke, Jack Cleere, Jennifer Cooper, Sarah Davey-Hull, Jo Dubiel, Robert Elms, Coral Flood, Jilly Forster, Noyumi Furukawa, Rose Harding, Christina Oakley Harrington, Andrew Hulme, Pete King, Andy Lockwood, Michelle Malka, James Mannion, Maria, Barry Mason, Niall McDevitt, Bronwyn Murphy, Kevin Murphy, Lisa Murphy, Mani Navasothy, Paul Newman, Canon Andrew Nunn, Allison Pollard-Barber, Max Reeves, Aileen Richmond, David Risley, Giles Semper, Valerie Shawcross, Nick Stanton, Pauline Stockmans, Vee, Joanna Vignola, Michelle Watson, Sarah Abigail Weightman, Tom Weller, Ion Will, Caroline Wise, Anne Wolfe, Scott Wood, Raga Woods, Jacqui Woodward-Smith.

***

Aside from minor amendments, *The Vision Books* and *Glossolalia* are reprinted as in the first edition. *The Mystery Plays* include significant textual revisions - creating a more coherent dramatic narrative - whilst retaining the epic structure of the complete cycle.

There was a temptation to update the *Glossolalia* - to reflect how profoundly Southwark has changed in little more than a decade, to chart the unfolding of the magical work at Crossbones, and to provide fresh insights and interpretations. Yet to embellish this peculiar resource – part glossary, part grimoire, part guide-book to uncharted territories - would be to dilute its potency. It sprang from the same source as the poems and plays: a vision of Eternity revealed in a particular time and place. As William Blake reminds us, the Universal is expressed in its "minute particulars".

The Southwark Mysteries embodies a poetic vision, a mystical drama, an act of magic, a spiritual praxis, a life-changing work-in-progress. The work was received as a gift; it changed my life and will - Goose willing - outlive me. It lives whenever it is read or performed - and the creative power of The Goose invoked in shining emptiness...

Open pathways.

J.C., Southwark, 2011
www.crossbones.org.uk
www.southwarkmysteries.co.uk

Preface to the First Edition

The Liberty of the Clink dates back to 1107 AD, when the Bishop of Winchester was granted a stretch of the Bankside to the west of London Bridge, which lay outside the law of the City of London. Here, the Bishop controlled the brothels, or "stews". The Whores of The Liberty were known as "Winchester Geese"...

The Vision Books of *The Southwark Mysteries* were revealed by The Goose to John Crow at Crossbones and Mary Overie dock, as recorded in my notebook on the night of 23 November 1996. My shamanic double had somehow raised the Spirit of a medieval Whore, licensed by a Bishop, yet allegedly denied Christian burial:

> For tonight in Hell
> they are tolling the bell
> for the Whore that lay at the Tabard,
> and well we know
> how the carrion crow
> doth feast in our Crossbones Graveyard.

The night I transcribed these lines, I presumed that "Crossbones" was The Goose's invention, a fittingly piratical name for a Whore's graveyard. Searching for clues in our local studies library, I discovered that it was an old name for the unconsecrated Magdalene or "single women's" burial ground in Redcross Way. I traced the site, to find that London Underground was in the process of digging it up. In the summer of 1998, I received confirmation that Museum of London archeologists had removed some 148 skeletons, including a "young woman's syphilitic skull with multiple erosive lesions, from Red Cross Way, Southwark". In my own back yard, ripped by drills and mechanical diggers. In the last days of the second millennium. "In London at the Temple of Isis." Dismembered fragments of a Secret Knowledge.

The work is to piece it together.

Researching the contents of *The Vision Books*, which in turn informed the writing of *The Mystery Plays* and *Glossolalia*, I had frequent recourse to the King James Bible, *The Nag Hammadi Library* edited by James M. Robinson, *English Mystery Plays* edited by Peter Happe, *An Encyclopaedia of London* edited by William Kent (1937 edition) and *The Concise Oxford Dictionary of the Christian Church* edited by E. A. Livingstone. Among the many other books I found useful and illuminating were Robert A. Armour's *Gods and Myths of Ancient Egypt*, E. J. Burford's *The Bishop's Brothels*, Martha Carlin's *Medieval Southwark*, Susan Haskins' *Mary Magdalen*, Stuart Holroyd's *The Elements of Gnosticism*, Elisabeth Moltmann-Wendel's *The Women Around Jesus*, Elaine Pagels' *Adam, Eve and the Serpent* and Gamini Salgado's *The Elizabethan Underworld*.

I am profoundly grateful to my partner Katharine Nicholls, my literary agent Nicki Stoddart, my publisher James Hogan and all at Oberon Books, for their unwavering faith in The Goose and her works. Barry Kyle was advisor to *The Mystery Plays*. Claudia Boulton, Ken Campbell and Di Sherlock each provided invaluable feedback on the work-in-progress.

Not forgetting Adam @ the Drome, Susan Aderin, John Adrian, Jane Arrowsmith, Roy Bendry, William Blake, William Burroughs, Stuart Caine, Canon Peter Challen, Chris and Emily, Fraser Clark, Nick Constable, Suzy Crowley, Libba Davies, Russ Denton, Tom Deveson, Nell Dunn, Peter Fitzgerald, Michaela and Bob Frost, Dave Gibbs, Robert Godley, Al Green, Green Angels, Paul Herbert, Dr Albert Hoffman, Evelyn Honig, Simon Hughes MP, George Isherwood, Canon Jeffrey John, Jane Jones, John Joyce, Juliet and Tom, Richard Kilgour, Duncan Law, Jahnet de Light, Liz and Con, Francine Luce, Hettie Malcomson, Tony Maples,

Michele McLusky, Jeff Merrifield, Clodagh O'Reilly, Dr Tuppy Owens, Conor Paterson, Irving Rappaport, James Richmond, Len Riley, Guy Rowsten, Mark Rylance, Iain Sinclair, Caroline Shepherdson, the Rev Richard Truss, the Very Rev Colin Slee, Stefan Szczelkun, Wilfred van Dorp, Anne Wolfe, Zanna…

And Kwan Yin, Goddess of Mercy.

"May all beings be free from suffering."

J.C. Southwark, 1999

THE VISION BOOKS

In Southwerk at the Tabard as I lay
Redy to wenden on my pilgrymage...

The Canterbury Tales by Geoffrey Chaucer

The Book of The Goose

I was born a Goose of Southwark
by the Grace of Mary Overie,
whose Bishop gives me licence
to sin within The Liberty.
In Bankside stews and taverns
you can hear me honk right daintily,
as I unlock the hidden door,
unveil the Secret History.

I will dunk you in the river
and then reveal my Mystery.

And when our Lords in Westminster
denounce my "Impious Blasphemy",
my gob in the face of all God-fearing
servants of His Majesty.
What though they throw me in The Clink,
or King's Bench or Marshalsea,
and leave me there to rot, they think,
for brazen acts of harlotry?

I call upon my Bishop
as Defender of my Liberty.

When all-mighty City Fathers,
those dread Guardians of Morality,
do ban "all gaming, drunkenness
and acts of gross effrontery".
What though they thunder Over There?
It matters not a fig to me.
Over 'ere's The Ward Without
The Law of London City,

where Whores are subject only to
fair Southwark and Her Liberty.

O, Over There, you'd swear
they were the image of propriety,
but row 'em Over 'ere, dear,
and it's all rape and pillage
and bondage and buggerage
with molly boys – "What jolly boys!" –
and Goose girls underage,

taking Liberties, and licence, dear.
We all have to deal with 'em.
We pump them and paddle them
and into bed we squeal with 'em.

"Let's all go bait the bear!"
        What madcap tomfoolery –
if it wasn't in the service of such a
pox-ridden Majesty.

Believe me, dear, been 'ere before
in all me pomp and finery,
with Johnny Wilkes and Dashwood
and the Lords of Hell-Fire Devilry,
when Southwark's Whores disported
in the habit of a nunnery
at Wycombe, in the Hell-Fire Caves,
that Chapter House of Liberty,

when Southwark's Mob took up the cry,
and the cry was "Wilkes and Liberty".

And when I hear those Hypocrites
decrying and denying me,
who make of me the vessel
of all known Vice and Depravity –
the way they talk, I swear you'd think
I was the Whore of Babylon,
as they make of me an altar
they see fit to rape my children on.

And a Minister of Morals –
O dear me, O what a carry-on.
Over There it's all The Family
and go on and marry on,
but when they're Over 'ere, dear,
then every Dick and Harry on
the front bench has some wench
or rough trade from Borough laid,

and every Mag Witch
in Shoreditch
has been poor St Mary Overied.

And did they think my ghosts
would not start kicking
against the poxy pricks
what a-done all the pricking?

How could they ever think
they could sanitise me,
dress up my Clink
to decriminalise me?

Turn me into their Heritage Theme Park?

"Over 'ere, dear, want to take
a walk down me dark
alleyways and doorways down me
blood fanny streamin'?"

Then it's – ooops!

Jack Sheppard
with his silver blade gleaming,

and it's one more body ditched
in Thames water
dreaming.

Yes I been 'ere before, dear,
oft'times in chastened circumstance.
I lay with Master Geffrey
at the Tabard, making dalliance

afore wending on his Pilgrimage
to tell a Tale of Canterbury,
and I rode out beside him
as the Childe of Mary Overie,

went riding for a Vision,
a Vision of Humanity,
Man, God and Beast communing
for one moment in Eternity.

And the healing of the sick,
and the Questioning Divinity
who asks Herself "What am I
to permit such wanton misery?"

And Compassion for all Souls that dwell
in shadows of mortality
compelling Her to take on very
flesh of that infirmity,

until She's born a crafty whore,
stewed in a Southwark hostelry,
and using all Her wherewithal
to take a Pilgrim's fancy,

and lay with him and play with him,
and open eyes to see
the Goddess that on Judgement Day
shall stand by Man and make his Plea.

And I was in that Miller's Wife,
who pushed her tush at Absalon,
who'd kissed he many a wench's lip,
but ne'er he such a hairy one.

You don't know me yet, dear.
You will, dear, I promise you.
I am a tricksy tart, dear.
My aim is to astonish you.

John Crow's Riddle

John Crow with a riddle in a madcap rhyme
here to reveal my Mystery
in London Town at the End of Time
John he go down on History.

John Crow in Cathedral Yard
cursed with my gift of Prophecy
here to play one last wild card
for Southwark and Her Liberty.

With a hey ho, jolly Jack Crow
and his merry merry band of outlaws O
never stumble when he trips
mad clown of the Apocalypse.

And some go "O ho! Who be this John Crow? This no
body rootless shaman O
kicking loose heels as the rank weeds grow
wild in our Southwark haven."

Then the crow on the gargoyle caw caw caw
and he draw John a map of infinity
where God rejoices more in the brazen Whore
than in the Wife in her pinch-faced Chastity.

With a knick knack paddywhack
give the dog a bible-black
John Crow whores a-hollerin',

in the sack on yer back
give the skull a good crack
see if it's a hollow 'un,

click-clack click-clack
don't look back
to see if Death's a-followin'.

For tonight in Hell
they are tolling the bell
for the Whore that lay at the Tabard,
and well we know
how the carrion crow
doth feast in our Crossbones Graveyard.

With a hey ho, jolly Jack Crow
and his merry merry band of outlaws O
never stumble when he trips
mad clown of the Apocalypse.

By the Grace of Our Lady Mary Overie

let them see

them that sell their time
to earn a daily crust to feed a family
them that trade the Future
in stocks and bonds, or speculate in property
them that crunch the numbers
on the number crunching north bank in the old City
then flood back 'cross London Bridge
to take their trains to Gravesend and the Estuary

let them see

in the hungry eyes of debtors
doing time with Dickens' father in Marshalsea
the denizens of Bedlam
now entrusted to the Care of our Community
the homeless in the subway
and the dead-end kids from Old Kent Road to Bermondsey
in the skull-faced Queers and Junkies
and the Tart who tested positive for HIV

the shining eyes of Our Goddess of Mercy

in the haggard face of John Crow
who watches from his high tower in Trinity
as in the single mother
who lives across the road at Number 23
the check-out girl in Superdrug
whose name-tag says her name is Charity
and in every human face that is
pocked and scarred by what we call Reality

by the Grace of Our Lady Mary Overie
let them see
the shining eyes of Our Goddess of Mercy

Three Four

let war
       be waged Without
break down the door and out the prison wall
let it all fall down to be born again at Liberty

and let Within
       the Dream of Skin
S/he that is without Sin cast the stone for we all
have our stake in the sum of human misery

our messes and scraps
       and clap traps
those niggling
naggling fibbety-gibbety
novelty grovelty mincey queeney
artsy fartsy – ooh! how nasty!
Minister watch your private partsy

party political
       put piggy in the middle
jump and hump and dump on him
pump him full of oestrogen
put a time bomb under him
Roast Pork and Bacon Fat
how'd you like to chew on that?

down my Ministry of Sound
where we do we tribal dances dear
what comes from underground
isn't subject to the Rule of Fear
it must've given you a start
to find me so lysergic dear
when it comes to stealing hearts
and healing rifts between our hemispheres
there's no trick I wouldn't pull
to entice you

Over 'ere

The Goose's Prophecy

I tricked mad John Crow
when he was in his ecstasy
to lend Me his voice
to make known My Prophecy

That in the month July
and the day shall be twenty-three
in the Year of Our Lady
Mary Overie
Southwark shall arise
naked in Her Liberty
on the South Bank of the Thames
arrayed in all Her finery
with all Her Children
endowed with grace and dignity
the deformed and the deviant
embraced into Her Unity

with Lambeth below Her
Blake's garden in Eternity
She shall open Her loins
to make hole the concavity
She'll shuffle two right click
then shuffle left another three
She'll strip the decks for one last
Sacred Profanity

And the Hypocrite shall blanch:
"Does She sanction such depravity?
The Great Whore of Revelation
is not that surely She?"

Relax, dear, you're Over 'ere,
don't go bustin' an artery
or poisoning me rivers with yer
self-loathing fartery.

The Body we all know, dear,
is privy to mortality.
This Flesh shall rot and wither,
as you're so fond of reminding me.

And when Your Kind's done,
when you're done despoiling me,
when you've had yer fun, son, you've
no further use for me.

So pipe down, shut yer mouf,
show some respect, humility,
and harken to that silence what is
brimming with immensity

Unspeakable

shall speak and in One Word
unfold Her Mystery

pronounce the End of Time
and beginning of Eternity

and all Her Children gathered there
in all their multiplicity

with One Voice
shall speak Her Name

And Her Name is Liberty

The Book of The Crow

There's a bridge of stone
And a bridge of iron
Gird the dock of St Mary Overie.
There's a Southwark Goose
With a Crow let loose
In the Heart of the ancient Liberty.

Led him down by the Clink
Through the sweat and the stink
Of the Stews to a Bankside Oratory,
And they saw the tide turn,
And they saw London burn,
Saw it rise from the ashes of History.

Then she led John Crow
To the river below
And her look was wanton and wild, and he
Saw through the grime
And the ruin of Time
The face of the Child, Eternity.

Then she gave him a look
That by hook or by crook
She would make him her Man: Brother Man, quoth she,
Come heal thy sickness,
Cleanse thy voice
And I'll have you to sing of my Mystery.

Come drain me Marsh
And tan me hide,
Come Immigrant and Refugee,
Come brew me beer
And wool be dyed
In the making of The Liberty.

Come lock and stock
To Overie Dock
From Flanders, France and Italy,
Come Molls and Dolls
And fol-de-rols
A-taking of The Liberty.

Come Heretic, Outlaw,
Jack Crow and Jack Daw,
Here shall ye all find Sanctuary,
Where the Actors and Whores
Are the Keepers of Doors
That open into The Liberty.

Come Black, come White,
We Open All Night.
In the Dance of Delight, all's One to me.
Take each as I find,
And I'll have them Mind
The Stewardship of My Liberty.

For true, this place
Has its brute ugly face
Of tribal bile and bigotry.
A Mob is turned,
A church is burned,
All in the name of Liberty.

We torched the Clink.
We wanted a drink.
We looted a gin distillery.
We ranted and reeled
In St George's Fields
And bloodied the face of Liberty.

And the Truth is hoary.
And the Truth is hard.
And the walls that are daubed with excrement
Say "True, if you shit
In your own back yard,
Then It shall be thy Testament."

Then she turns her Crow's eye
To a Bankside sty
With the spit of the fat of the Goose in the Stew,
And the Bear in the Pit
And the Dogs at it
And the Evil they know not that they do.

Sez: 'ere by the sluice
Of a Goose's juice
Let all enjoy my hospitality,
But a pox and a curse
On the ignorant Nurse
Who suckles such lock-jawed brutality.

Our heads were shorn,
In carts were drawn
Through howling Mob's humbuggery,
Through sticks and stones –
God rest these bones
Now safe within The Liberty.

And the whipping boy,
The Jew and the Goy,
And the Printer put in the pillory,
We shall wipe clean his face,
For it is no disgrace
To be whipped in the service of Liberty.

The punk and the ponce
And the John Crow dunce
And the broken-wing John Crow deformity,
Them that stumble and trip
Shall have Citizenship
And Equal Rights under The Liberty.

Them that hop, flit and flap
Like birds in a trap,
Them that crouch in a house of rats fearfully,
In the feeble and frail
And the Nightingale
Who sang in the House of Liberty.

In the letting of blood
In the Bermondsey mud,
In the leech in St Thomas' infirmary,
In the dumb that talk
And the Dead that walk
And keep the Night Watch in the Liberty.

In the church-pews and stews
They whisper the news,
The ghost of an old Goose's Heresy –
That the Magdalene Whore
A love child bore
To the dancing Lord of The Liberty.

And I was in that
Magdalene Whore
Who walked the streets of Bermondsey,
I traded hard
In every yard
To keep the Child at Liberty.

To Margaret's Fair
With Bull and Bear,
With Mummers' Masque and Mystery,
Poor Actors fret
And strut and sweat
The takings of The Liberty.

Then a Theatre torn down
In Shoreditch Town
And over the river the timbers row,
And 'ere in the Pit
And the reek of it
They are building for me my Wooden O.

Then the World's a Stage
And in these Holy Days,
If you will come with me, John Crow,
I will show you my face
And a secret place,
The same I once showed Master Willie O.

Now all the World knows
And the World may abhor
But the World cannot unmake Poetry:
God's Actor is bedfellow
Here with God's Whore
In the Sacred Heart of God's Liberty.

Come Trickster, Shaman,
Prophet and Fool,
Speaking in tongues of The Mystery.
Let all men contend,
But God defend
The lineaments of My Liberty.

Come snake and whistle
And rattle and drum,
Come open me Cavern in Jubilee,
Come open me Tomb
To crackle and boom,
And let the Bells ring in The Liberty.

Come Christian and Jew,
Muslim, Buddhist, Hindu,
Let each to His own True Divinity.
Let even the blind
Material Mind
Walk His own hallowed path in Liberty.

And seek not to bind
The Visions you find
In naming the parts of The Mystery.
In naming the part
Don't miss the Heart,
The Heart of My Holy Liberty.

Though you trick me up
As Virgin or Whore
And make me debase right bestially,
I am the Dancing
Child, the Door
That opens into Eternity.

And by Blackfriars Ditch,
Old John he twitch:
What I want to know, sez John: Is why me?
And The Goose she smiles,
She sez: Woman's wiles.
You and me, dear, we been 'ere before, sez she.

And it's the old shabby score,
The John and the Whore,
The Six Steps to Heaven and the Easy Ride,
But now it's just you and me
And the salt of the sea
And Today you do pay me to be your Guide.

So unto this place
On a wild Goose chase
I've led you a merry dance, sez she,
And you followed the trail
And may live to tell the tale
Of a friend of a friend
Of The Liberty.

I am John Crow

and The Goose is my Muse

She maketh me to waketh
in my walking talking shoes

Cross Bones to Clink
by Mary Overie dock

by the third cock's crow
by the third crow's cock

may the Spirit be with Crow
and all them that walk beside him

when he walk about the Liberty
with but his Goose to guide him.

John Crow Trickster

No Preacher

and if he ever done so
John Crow done defrock
Man done reap as he sow

when Preacher Man make war
on the Witch and the Whore
Puritan done for Crow

Oliver Cromwell done for Crow
when he shut down The Goose and her Wooden O

stripped and whipped him at the cart's arse
from Bedlam to Cross Bo'

stuck he head on a spike
to feed the carrion crow

panic attack
now John Crow back
a-wheelin' and a-dealin' wid he
hungry Ho

now Crow break cover
wid he Harlots and he Witches
he say: dub me Dog of God
I bin 'ere with me Bitches,

O so purty playin' dirty
in them bridle and split britches
them the Daughters of Arachne
puttin' in the scarlet stitches.

DING-
DONG

they come
Moll Cut Purse and Merry Mad Maud
and Sha Manic Tom
o' Bedlam

with John Crow and he Whore
bangin' on Cathedral Door
they back for more than just a pious
sermon.

So...

Goose sez to Crow

John,
riddle me low
riddle me your quick-quick
slow thing

your Waterman row
Thames river flow

riddle me A Do about
an O Thing.

by the third cock's crow
by the wooden

O

i do not deny her di V inity

and in the d E ad of night

fea R not for i know

i walk I n the hallowed

light of h E r liberty

The Ballad of Mary Overie

Mary Overie
her Old Man ran a ferry O
man so miserly
he thought he'd save a penny O
if he could fool his family
that he was dead
alas poor
Mary
O
Lady of The Liberty
Goose and Crow

so Old Man Overie
he put the word a-round O
Bankside down to Bermondsey
that he had gone and drowned O
a-tumbled from his Thames ferry
and so is dead
alas poor
Mary
O
Lady of The Liberty
Goose and Crow

then Old Man Overie
crept home by dead of night O
sees not what he expects to see
his house is full of light O
sees merriment and revelry
not one tear shed
alas poor
Mary
O
Lady of The Liberty
Goose and Crow

when Old Man Overie
returning from the dead O
burst in on his family
they bashed him on the head O
they thought he was a ghost now he
is well and truly
dead, poor
Mary
O
Lady of The Liberty
Goose and Crow

Mary Overie
she come into the money O
True Love eagerly
come riding for to marry O
was thrown and fell most grievously
another dead
alas poor
Mary
O
Lady of The Liberty
Goose and Crow

Then Mary Overie
she took it for a sign O
to found a Bankside Priory
to heal the Wound Divine O
reveal God's Ways of Mystery
and raise the Dead
O blessed
Mary
O
Lady of The Liberty
Goose and Crow

and she led him down to the mudflats

by the red bridge at Blackfriars
over from St Bride's, Brid
who turned water to beer in all Ireland,

and remembered her own bog-
Irish come to drain the marsh,
to dyke and dam, shore up
Roman ditch and causeway,

reclaiming land as yet unfit
for human habitation,
Dirty Lane and Bandyleg
Walk, hovels and

churches torched by King Mob
rampant, and the secret Mass
House in Kent Street where the rats
rustled their prayers like parchment,

fistful of Thames mud
let slip
and wash away.

she was the girl

in Jacob's
        cholera in-
        fested slum

the one who saw
        there could be more
        to life than this

as when her Lord
returning from the Dead

she touched and healed his wounds
retrieved him with a kiss.

LONDINI AD FANUM ISIDIS

Here Isis wept
in Thames river mud
for her children sold into bondage
in slave-mart by River of Babylon,
Queenhithe to Gropecunte Lane.

Here Rome converts
to cannibalise in Bull and Creed,
Body of Christ spitting and touretting
where Tooley the torturer
slews down Crucifix Lane.

Here Magdala
returned in Overie,
Body of the Whore washed clean
in St Thomas culvert, dunked in the River
and rose again.

The Book of the Egyptian

As in Israel come out of Egypt
so in Egypt come out of Rome
the ferryman's daughter
fetched up Over 'ere
two thousand light year from home.

With her Tarot pack and the shirt off her back
and her one-string fiddle and squeeze-
box, her shuffles and clicks
and her fiddlesticks
and her map of the Mysteries.

And she has been 'ere this two thousand year
on the Banks of Thame-Isis in Overie
in her asses milk bath
with her cackling laugh
in the Clink with her skeleton key.

With a widdishins jig
she go rip the rig.

The Goose is loose in The Liberty.

here John Crow and i read

the sign at the pilgrim's inn

don't have to be
broken to be blessed
by Overie.

here John Crow and i found
larking in Thames
mud the broken
mask of god
SIVA SAKTI.

here John Crow and i pray
Goddess of Mercy
heal
these broken wings
within me.

The Mystery of George and Martha

Mary O'Reilly
tell me Mary Martha Mystery
in the Yard of George's hostelry

George
of Dragon notoriety
patron saint of nationality
did pierce the Dragon bodily
with his fearsome Lance of Destiny

and Martha
tamed it tenderly
stroked the head and cunningly
with her girdle bound the beastie
and so did harness Dragon energy

According to O'Reilly
in the Yard of George's hostelry

and I the Child at Liberty
to reveal My Southwark Mystery

how George
returned to Liberty
to tend the very Dragon he
had slain, did labour patiently
to heal the wound of History

once
and for all eternity

by the Grace of Mary Overie.

George and the Dragon Rap

O George he was a soldier
who refused to follow orders
and he had the Roman Empire in a flap,

so God knows how Georgie
got done in that Roman orgy
and then stitched up with this Dragon-killing rap.

For when Rome at last converted
our George's hands got dirtied
as Defender of an Empire that was rotten to the core,

George the Emperor's appeaser
rendered Christ unto his Caesar
took the High Priestess of Egypt and he made of her the Whore.

Then George he went crusading
a-reaping and a-raiding
and he slaked his trusty blade in Dragon gore,

in the Temple of Jerusalem
the Children of the Saracen
got carved up on the altars of his god-damned Holy War.

Then as George came down in History
he fell in with bad company
they dressed him up in Gordon's bigots' clothes,

with their Roast Beefs and Bully Boys
a-marching making mighty noise
to George's Fields to bloody Patrick's nose.

And George was all too willing
to take their thirty shilling
for to go a Dragon-killing for their sluttish English Rose,

and the Mob made him the stronger
dinged the Dragons with his donger
then he chopped 'em up and fed 'em to the crows.

Now George, seeing the error
of his ways did flee in terror he
took refuge in the hospice of St Mary Overie,

where Sister Martha did receive him
nursed him through his gruesome grieving
then they set about the healing

of the Dragon
slain in the name of England
St George and Liberty.

Southwark Crown Court
3rd April 1998

True M'lud
we know all about the Borough Boys
but this is no ordinary case of Missing
Body Parts

these heretics harbour no relics
there are no crosses in their boneyard no
fingers in the deep freeze no tell-tale
Bleeding Hearts

the evidence is purely circumstantial
unconfirmed reports
a Cross fell out of the blue
on Bermondsey

some monk from the Abbey
sounds more like a case
of Care
in the Community

be that as it may
we have reason to believe
there may be grounds for charges
of conspiracy

in the literal sense M'lud
a "breathing together"
Communion of Whores the Outlaw
Rites of Mary Overie

in repetition of a well-
turned Spell

by bell
book and guttering candle

in tongues by secret
pathways walked and spoken aloud

blood-
bandaged echo
Magdalene whisper
in the empty shroud.

Here

2000 Years
mouth stopped with a stone
in the belly of a well
in Mary Overie.

2000 Years of Empire
2000 Years of X-rated
Flesh did not defile
The Daughter of Eternity.

Here Magdala in Overie
reveals Her Goose's Heresy
in Thames mud larking
with the Child born at Liberty.

Here Jesus walks
on the Sea of Galilee
laughter echoes
in the Garden of Gethsemene.

The Book of The Constable

In the Year Ninety Six
God was up to His tricks
in Southwark at work
in a Crow and a Goose
to fetch Rylance and Slee
an old rusty key
to open a door
let the Spirit loose.

Thus as Provost did pray
for a Mystery Play –
Cathedral and Globe –
so The Goose and The Crow
a Liberty took
with the Constable's book
and thus it was thus
and so it was so.

And God put 'em all 'ere
for a reason, dear
and in Southwark he set 'em
'twixt cant and cantrips
foundations to shake
and on the Day make
a drama of His
Apocalypse.

O
        but let's not go
getting too big for our
bankside booties
                dear.

ego?
        ergo
punch and judy show
where's the constable?

                "over 'ere."

now the constable's a vegetarian
but 'as been known to eat 'er meat.
Times like this I sez to 'er, dear
yer really can't be too effete
cuz When The Bottom Drops Out
                my sweet
there'll be No More Time
to whinge and moan.
yer asks me wot I likes to eat?
Roast Beef On The Bone.

The Bankside Book of Revelation

i.

In the Book of the Law,
some John carve up some Whore
with the Mark of the Beast, in some
Bottomless Pit.

Take a New John Sha Man
to carry the can,
slop out Old John's
bucket of shit.

Take more than Wormwood
to open this Door.
Take more than Death
and His Dogs of War.

Take a Sha Manic Crow
to Master he Goose
when that Last Trump blow
Lord, when all Hell break loose.

Take a Crow on the juice
in the Boneyard to know
when to hold he Wild Goose
and when to let go.

ii.

Take a Goose and a Crow
to shuffle the deck

in the kiss of the Beast
when He nuzzle We neck
as here in We Harlot
who hold He in check

in We Trick of We Trade
in We bushel and peck
in We Alchemist Gold
in We Ghetto Boy dreck

in We Nick the Greek
in We Mehmet the Turk
in We Flesh Be Weak
in We Make It Work

in We Mother and Child
in We turn trick to feed
in We wanton and wild
in You

Prick Us
We Bleed.

iii.

Just what exactly is it you want, Lord?
What do you want from me?

I can play the horny hag
you can tie me up and gag me
but for Christ's sake, let the Child
go free.

How do you want me? Down on all fours
in The Land of The Lord of The Slum?

In the Darkness At Noon?
O don't come too soon
Lord, let not Thy
Kingdom come.

iv.

Take a Vision revealed
in the Land of the Trinity
for the Beast to be healed
by The Goose at Liberty.

Crow Bitches say: Hey, Beast,
We got your Number.

Crow and he Witches' Yeast
take out that Number.

v.

Witchfinder, yo' Witch
got a new game to play.

She go cook up one last night
flight on She K.

She go look you in the eye
with She head full of sky.

She go see who blink first.
She go blow you away.

vi.

OK so maybe it's just
mad John Crow
in here with he old Goose bone.

So maybe there's Them
with their Brimstone and Fire
and their Judgement written in stone.

They got The Books
of the Law and the Beast.
They got the solid state.

We got The Bride
and the Wedding Feast
and We Wild Card at Heaven's Gate.

We got We Christ
and He Magdalene Whore
here to get off She Kit and petition

in the name of The Goose
on a wing and a claw
Father, grant We Thy Children admission.

vii.

Take a Goose and a Crow
in a Bankside show,

a Mad Tom and he Mad Maud
Madonna,

Take a Rig to rip
And a Whore to strip

and a Shaman to go down
on her.

But don't fret, my pet,
it's a family show.

There's nothing to upset
yer Mum.

It'll all be very
tastefully done

when We
IMMANENTIZE
THE ESCHATON.

viii.

and always

room for a laugh
even a dirty one,

always room for a goose
to be the flighty flirty one,

always room for a crow
even a broken one,

who seeks not to know
in the name of the Unspoken One,

always room for a Sin
in God's House in Overie,

room at the inn
for the Child
born at Liberty.

ix.

then let Crow pause for breath
to see his own death
prefigured in Southwark
Cathedral vaults,

but let him not blink
nor shudder nor shrink
from observing his own all-
too-human faults,

let Tempest not toss
when in the roof boss
the Devil doth lick his lips
greedily,

but let him pass through
in the name of the True
God and His consort
at Liberty,

let shed We snake skin,
let We all pass within
by the Grace of the Yin
in the Overie.

Liberty Zen

and if you happen
to run into the Buddha
down Borough High Street,

                    do 'im!

The Book of The New South Bank

i.

We splish
in the splash
of the New Bankside Power

We clash
in the flash
of the OXO Tower

We Hole in the Wall
to the Ministry Ball
and We know how to pack
a punch

We Clink and Red-
Cross Wicca and Dread
the Original Real
Wild Bunch.

ii.

We click
We clack
We Belles of the Borough
and up for the crack.

We get out We tits
for the rush and the glitz
and all We get is a smack in the face
and We finish up flat on We back.

We Sub
We Dom
We strippin' it off
We strappin' it on

We Earthly Delight
We do it All Night
Live Show
in the London DunJon.

We do it again
Down Skin Market Lane
until the Doing is Done.

iii.

We Rough
We Trade
don't mind the abuse
so long as it's paid

We wearin' big smile
as We dance in the aisle
as We wait for the lights to fade.

We clank
We clink
We salsa pumpin'
Bible thumpin'
Elephant Castle Pink.

We clink
We clank
We Rent and Yard is dirty and dank.

We got better things to do
than be work in a Stew
but We Do

We're the New
South Bank.

iv.

sow's ear
silk purse
We fête at the Tate
before We too Late
and We wind up the stiff
in the Damien Hearse.

We might look pretty sick
but when puss comes to prick
We don't dick with a Goose's Curse.

v.

We Trick
We Track
the drill and the jack-
hammer tear down We shack

rip up We stone
and rattle We bone
click clack Jack go
Pay It All Back.

We track
We trick
We clank
and clink
and shuffle
and click

We might play the Fool
but when pack comes to mule
we know how to pack
a kick.

vi.

We spin
We span
We smell the blood of a Vampire Man

he shall turn on the spit
when the shit
        hits
        the Pit

and the smart money hits
        the Fan.

We hip
We hop
We "Liberty Rules"
We know how to stay cool
in the heat
of a pressure

     drop

for We all done Time
in primordial slime
banged up with We bucket of slop.

vii.

We Eve
We Fall
We "Apple? Why not?"
We grovel in grot
We Try To Make Sense Of It All.

We Masque
We Mime
We all of We Souls
crawled out of We holes
to be born at the End of Time.

We Gyve
We Gyre
We John Crow
Mary O
and Southwark Cathedral choir.

We looking to do
the Water to you
before you go do We the Fire.

viii.

We honk
'til We hoarse
"O Lord
let Thy Goose
not stew in her juice
nor baste in Thy barbeque sauce."

We Crow
God's Clown
We "Ferryman ferry We
over to Overie
when the Last Screen go down.

Ferryman ferry We
over to Overie
take We to Liberty Town."

We Goose
God's Whore
We Goose and We Crow We
"Waterman row We
over the Other Shore.

Ferryman ferry We
over to Overie
open Cathedral Door."

ix.

We Kid
but We brave
We "Sir, if We may
come here to lay
Flowers on We
Mother's
Grave."

We meek
We mild
We Magdalene Whore
walk in We door
hand We She
Laughing
Child.

We "Listen! Right?
fair's fair.
Have done with Burning the Witch
and Baiting The Bear"
      "Yeah, I know she's
      a bit wild
      but just strip her down
      take her to Town –"
"for Christ's sake!
She's Only
a Child."

x.

Mad Tom
Mad Maud
"We come 'ere to cure
this Dragon of yore
wort slain by the Cross of St Jord."

Let Man of Straw
        no more wage War
                on the Beautiful Whore
when all She takes
        is a kiss on the stair
                by the light of an open door.

We shriven
We shrive
We struggle to mesh
in the Dream of the Flesh
while keeping the Spirit alive.

We lax
We loose
We Bishop and Tart
and a Way with a Heart
for a walk with a Crow and a Goose.

A Song of Innocence

There's a little private problem
not so very far from home
with a little plastic body
in a little plastic dome

for it hasn't got a heart
and it hasn't got a soul
and it hasn't got a part
and it hasn't got a hole

and how shall we yet live
how can we be reborn
unless we first forgive
the part whereof
each one
of us is
torn
?

Twilight of the Trade Marks

so we tried the Real World
and when it didn't take
we tricked it up and
clicked it up and
sold ourselves a clever Fake.

"Eternity £12,999"
(and cheap at the price)
This Year's Model of the Earthly Paradise.

and tonight looks like every John in town
down to Matthew Mark Luke
and me

is loitering with intent
Hell-bent
on branding
the key.

Sarf London catch a feel for the
Real Thing – Don't Buy into some Porno-Shop sim-
ulation

We Here In The Flesh
to reclaim and repossess
the Spirit and its Quest
for Consummation

want Real John Thing
not some poxy proxy Jack-potted
Cumalot and Co
cackola

want Free From Fear and the Systems
it spawned in the Mind of the
Great Con-
troller

and if the Priest of the Raven
or Imam block

they go Rock
and Roll Over.

BRITANNIA HOUSE with the HAZCHEM

warning recently removed, Old Ted
glassed in with his cobalt CCTV
and the smoke of his forty-a-night
     02:23

says the luminous dead
-eyed digital lizard
says SLEEP DON'T SLEEP toll
     the bell rattle the key

we're 'ere to Keep
The Night Watch
you and me
     All's Well.

Bridges

and crowds agape

        sky hawk
        crack-
                booming down on

        Towers
Southwark
Millennium
Blackfriars
        Waterloo
        Hungerford
                Westminster
                Lambeth

as she turns her Crow's eye
to the Thames rip-tide
and the bright City lights, immutably
mutable, shifting,
the river-mud sifting
Birth Rites of the 21st Century.

kateEkaos

lost rivers
bedded and threaded through her

where geese duck and dive
let her waters revive and renew her

and in her wild places
i will love honour and defend her

and walk with her
in this cloud of unknowing

hold and release
in her coming and going

and rejoice
in the Great Unknown

who send her.

Gaia

hey-
diddle-diddle
the cat and the fiddle
I riddle me Goose's song

if God's the Man
with the Master Plan

who's the Dark Eyed Girl
who just lets it unfurl

who's making It up
as It goes along?

Yab Yum

i.

hermaphrodite
gods in the stairwell
playing
peek-a-boo

with all of us sat
stumped
punching the keys
watching the screens go down

as the last train
out of town
pulls out
of Waterloo

ii.

and if J. Crow's Muse
not crackle her fuse
when she cockle him cruse of pottage

and if her face
in hyperspace
be not whited out with wattage

and we no more fixate
on the form and the state
that shutteth us down from infinity

False God of the Head
at last pronounced Dead

to unmask
the True
Human
Divinity

Post Script

And here's poor Dr Dworkin
Still packing his pork in
The God on the slab
In his bunker.
With his selfish gene
He's so moody & mean.
He's a real millennial spunker.

The Book of The Honest John

John Crow
he throw
>seven clicks on he
>HO
card in a phone-box
routine:
>J. CROW SHAMAN
>WANTS TO TRADE TRICKS
>WITH THE TANTRIC
>LIBERTY QUEEN.

Jahnet? Hello.
It's me, John Crow –
we met at the SFC.
With my Goose makin' play
I am callin' to say
you makin' connection
in me.

Now as I am John Crow Shaman
I must to my Goose be true
but when I honour Her Light
in the Ladies of the Night
I delight to divine Her
in you.

and as a Man in the business of Healing
this 2000 year stinkin' Stew
with my clicks and my sticks –
what d'ya say – we trade tricks?
You and me, girl – we got
work
to do.

True I comin' on strong –
but not like some John
go take in the name of the Giver.
Jahnet, hear me through –
I am sayin' to you
that this John
For True
Can Deliver.

Jahnet sez: You come
to the right place, John
no don't be afraid –
I don't bite –

if you're lookin' to Heal
if you're playin'
For Real
John
I am Jahnet
de Light.

So, John, how you been?
Looks like you seen
things that've left you
ragged and raw

but if you For Real
about comin' to Heal
then you must
leave your
Cross
at the door.

she sez: things like this only
happen in the movies – the
prodigal John and the Whore –
the Beauty, the bait
and the blind
date with fate –
one last chance to settle
the score.

So before we begin
to unravel the Skin
two basic house-rules
John
CONSENTING ADULTS
NO COERCION.
Got it? We here to
have fun.

O come
          into
my Healing Room
my burgundy lace Confessional
- no, don't try to get cute, just
                    let JAH NET reroute,
relax, John
you're with a professional.

let's try it like this...

let's try essential oil
in the green dragon bowl.

let's try the lights down low
let's try the orange glow.

let's try the altar-cloth
purple and crimson.
am I getting you off?

let taste in thy lips
the blood
fruit of Eden.

let's climb the spiral stair-
way to heaven.
am I getting you there?

let's try blood-
red candles and red
satin sheets on the bed.
(tissues, in case you
foam at the mouth when yuh
White Witch walk in yuh Head)

let's…

do Mag-Witch washing the Master's feet
then wiping them dry with her hair
let's try I
anointing Thy Body
let's do the Truth and the Dare.

let's try We Turn On The Lights
then fade them back down to dim
let's try the blind-
fold the butterfly stroke
let's do the Her and the Him.

let's try O
you like that, John Crow?
just say Yes to one moment
Heaven sent
Jahnet goin' down
on the Real John Town
a-humpin' and a-bumpin'
in the Ballroom of Enlightenment.

let's do THE DUNGEON
I am Thy Mistress –
THOU SHALT NOT SPUNK
until I grant Thee permission.

done WAR ON FLESH
now what do ya say
we try LOVING IT INTO
SUBMISSION?

let's do BREATH
         slip-
          streaming lip
          to lip
let's do a Little Death.

let's – no, John, don't go slack –
let's do whatever it takes –
let's try the Arab strap – let's – no
DON'T HAVE A HEART ATTACK

let's…

let's NOT TRY not to try
let's just let ourselves
let's let live and learn to forgive
and forget ourselves.

let's just GET OUT OF THE FUCKING WAY –
let IT do what IT has to do –
NO ME
NO YOU –
only the Dance
in the Trick of the Trance –
let's make the Mudra
          SIVA
          SAKTI.

ONE
MORE
TIME
      let's

do it loud and dirty
come on do it to me hard
let's do it where the wild dogs howl
in our
          CROSS
          BONE
          YARD.

When Crow and Merry Whore
get to banging on the floor
when they wham bam slam-
dunkin' on the ceiling

when they make the boards crack
when they Beast with Two Back
when they switch back the track
from Thought to Feeling

when the Big O hits
it's not all just
cocks and clits
this is Shaman's Work
seeing is revealing

this is where we put back
the Missing Bits
here in this
Her House
of Healing.

Well, that's that done
John, get your kit on –
alright, you can
watch me wash –

you got 35
'til the next John arrive
don't want you to scare 'im
      'e's posh.

Now you know how John Crow
does honour he HO
and is only in Her Name
he so forgiving.

Thank Goddess
Thank Luce
when She turn Her Crow loose
to root with Her Goose in the living.

When The Goose and The Crow
finally let go
as above so below
                go melt like butter.

more to Vision than the Eye
more to Fuck than Spanish Fly
more to Chaos than the butterfly
                flutter.

Star-light, Star bright
a path for a Crow
and his Goose's flight
                a window
                in to
                the sky.

JAH NET: John, there is one
thing we have to agree
before we can start anew
that the Whore that you strip
for the lash of the whip
that Whore, as in me, is in you.

I know it – sez John:
it takes one to know one
and we all done been here before.
When all's said and done
I done been that John
and God knows I been that Whore.

John Crow and his Mawdelyn Whore
here to catch as catch can.
Here to strike Dread
in the pit-
bull head
and heart of the Dominator Man.

So Geese, tell your Johns
tell 'em each every one
your Bishop, your Judge, your MP
tell 'em: stop playin' games
or it's time to name names
It is Time to ReClaim The Liberty.

and Jahnet sez: Whoa!
Easy, John Crow.
Don't go nursing that old
righteous grudge.

Be not so hard on
thy Brother Broken John.
JUDGE NOT THAT YE BE NOT
JUDGED.

Do you think you can tomcat
the Mysteries?
You want to Trade Mark
The Unknown?

Man it's Time to ReLease
every one of my Geese
got a mind and a Will
and a honk of her own.

and Jahnet sez: O
it's nice being a Muse,
though we all know The Goose holds the key.

John Crow, don't show
all your cards in one throw.
– sez crafty Jahnet to me.

House Of Correction?

all smoke and
        mirrors, dear

here we pierce to purify
the Flesh
        here – and O…
        here

        set FREE
        FROM FEAR.

CONSENTING ADULTS

read the sign, dear.
If you want something else
you've no business here

though you never know what you might find

you say that Southwark
is only a place
I say She's a State
of Mind.

The Book of The Game

i.

It's After Hours
in the Eden Bar.
Here's Eve and The Man.
Here's The God With No Name.
He's horny. He's hunky.
He smells like a skunk. He's
The Player. He's The One and Only Game.

And Eve, you can bet
she's willing and wet.
She's all over Him.
Man, that Woman no shame.
She pampers and strokes Him
and laughs at His jokes
like they all know it's only a Game.

And The Man sez: uh-oh.
Man sez: Here we go.
sez: Next thing we know
He'll be sorry He came.
If God has His Way
there'll be All Hell To Pay
for playing along with His Game.

But God sez: Is cool,
Man, I make the House Rule.
Are you in The Picture,
or are you in The Frame?
Sez: You welcome to stay,
but we play it My Way.
You ready? Let's play The Game.

Then Eve starts to shake.
God hands her The Snake,
sez: Seek Not To Know
What Thou Art, Whence Thou Came.
and The Snake sez: Why not?
It'll sure help a lot
if we all know the Rules of The Game.

Then God, ruttish and raw,
get Eve on the floor,
and He give her What For
like He staking His claim.
When God get to spunk
The Man wake with a clunk
with his God on the nod and his Girl

on The Game.

ii.

Eve sez: Here
let candles be lit
let incense sweeten
the stink of The Pit.

Eve sez: What say
I mix us some Snake Bites?
We go swallow the venom.
We go go into Trance.

Man, stop looking so blue.
Let God do what God do.
Let's vamp it. Let's voodoo.
Let's let The Dead dance.

God sez: Darling Eve,
you almost make me believe
in a Bull-God who wrestles
His own Nature to tame.

Sez Eve: Tell me, dear!
We get 'em all 'ere,
the Man and the Beast
and their God of the Game.

Man sez: Excuse me
butting in on this spree,
not wishing to mince
words, or mangle or maim,

but some dumb Human trash
got to empty the ash-
trays, when you Two is done
with your Game.

Yes it's After Hours
in the Eden Bar.
Outside the whole damn
street up in flame.

Inside there's just God
and Eve and The Man
All for One, locked on
to The Game.

iii.

God sez: Man of Eve,
do you think I would leave
you alone Here to shoulder
the brunt of My blame.

I go shack up with you,
get to Work on this Stew
see what We can Do
with The Game.

I go live with the poor,
with the Man and His Whore,
the weak and the wounded,
the sick and the lame,

I go mourn My own loss
I go hang on My cross
I go beat My self at
My own Game.

Eve sez: God, don't die
without telling us why…

why we struggle for breath,
God, free us from Death…

We go open the Cave,
fetch God back from the Grave…

We go oil God's Body.
We go kindle His flame.
We go lay Him on the bed.
We go shake, go wake Him up.
We go Raise Him From The Dead.
We go Turn Every Trick in The Game
to balm and to heal His Wound, to reveal
the Human Face of The God With No Name.

I am the wind

I rake the wild grasses
I am the reaper, the sower, the seed.
I am the day of the bonny lads and lasses.
I am the night where their secret paths lead.

I am the sense-field. I flower in your fingers.
I am the musk in the dusk of the day.
I am the ghost of the smile that lingers
When the face where it flickered has faded away.

I am the song of the blackbird in Eden.
I am the waft in the butterfly wing.
And I am Here in the static and stutter
That shutter how much I and I can take in.

I am the White Noise of a Nervous System.
I am the Silence in which it reroutes.
I am the Gods and the Men who resist 'em,
The madness in the eyes of the Men In Suits.

I am in George. I must conquer my Dragon.
I am in Martha. I nurse the red gash.
I am hag Ceridwen with Her raw red rag on.
I am Kali, razor in the flash and slash.

I am the light in the shadow revealing.
I am the Grace that transfigures the Sin.
I am the Wound that prefigures the Healing.
I am the Light at the Travellers' Inn.

I'll be your icon, your Muse, your conceit.
I'll be whatever you would have me be.
I'll be Mary Magdalene washing your feet
If it helps you see through
What divides "you" from "me".

Now

John Crow said:
I go Raise The Dead,
walk the old crooked track
with my poor stricken Goose.

and Jah Net said: John,
There Are No Dead.
You ready? Let's
turn 'em loose.

The Book of The Magdalene

Here
The Song Of A Beautiful Whore

Her Name
was Southwark
and I in her lay

one night
along the Pilgrim's Way.

O

come
to me come
in to me come
take me from the South

come
Man of Wal
skin blue with woad
and strange tongues in thy mouth

from
Honor Oak
to Camber Well
where cripples dance for joy

come
Sons of
Taliesen lovely
doomed and laughing boy

click
and we come
to the click
of a stick
and a shaman's drum

by rattle
bag of stones
by our old goose's bones
we walk our crooked mile to Kingdom Come

St Paul
beat a Pan
Sita beat a Ram Jam
OM MANI PADME
HUM

Now some church-going ladies of Dulwich
may blush at John Crow
and his Maudlin Whore.

The parts raw and red
they may wish left unsaid
and banished to some bottom drawer.

Then dream on, dear ladies
safe in your slumber,
heed not my knock at your door,

you can take the Whore
out of Southwark
but you'll never take Southwark
out of the Whore.

Entombed in the shadow of Bedlam:
The Imperial Museum of War.

In the Garden of Peace
The Winchester Geese
consort with Kwan Yin

and the Magdalene Whore.

In the wards of Old Guy's leaden tower,
in the Elephant and Castle sub-way
they graffiti her name,
She who comes to reclaim
the World that was taken away.

On the steps of St George the Martyr,
red-eyed and roaring, a bum
did totter and sway
and topple and splay
and stutter the words: She Is Come.

She is come out of Egypt by Greenwich
upriver, the Dogs to her right
along the black beach
around Limehouse Reach
with the City of London in sight.

In Cathedral Provost may ponder
if he should unbar the Great Door
with a wink and a nod
to the Glory of God
in the guise of an unredeemed Whore.

Let Bishop's crook offer him Counsel,
Ways and Means for the Door to unjam.
If needs must be seen
that the Whore be washed clean
of her Sin by the Blood of the Lamb,

then let it be so, but then let it go,
the Guilt and the Shame and the Sin.
Let go of the Law
that made her a Whore
and then, for God's sake, let her in.

Let in, let in, let no colour of skin
nor creed debar Other from ceremony.
Let the gong of Tibet
bong out an octet
with the Bells of St Mary Overie.

And Now It Is Time To Call

Time

Last orders, please!
Millennium?

Closing, gents,
come on, drink up!

Hurry up, please
the ferryman
is waiting down at Stew Lane steps
waiting to row you over, dear,

waiting to find you Over There

and so
to row you
Over 'ere.

The Pilgrim's Way

Let not the Letter of the Law
Deny the Spirit Liberty,
Nor burn my book of pictures
Which It take for rank idolatry,

For I am the Mistress Southwark,
Am the Daughter of Eternity,
And in me the Broken Man
Shall be made whole, as merrily

We wenden on our Pilgrimage,
Who knows what wonders yet to see
Along the winding track of Time
On our journey home from Canterbury.

THE MYSTERY PLAYS

The Southwark Cycle of Mystery Plays

The Southwark Mysteries was first performed in Shakespeare's Globe Theatre and Southwark Cathedral, on 23rd April 2000, by a combined professional and community cast.

JESUS, Roddy McDevitt
SATAN, Jacqueline Haigh
THE GOOSE, Di Sherlock
JOHN CROW, John Constable
JOHN TAYLOR, Niall McDevitt
MOLL CUTPURSE, Michelle Watson
YAHWEH, Peter Marinker
CROMWELL, Paul Hamilton
BEELZEBUB, Benji Reid

Director, Sarah Davey-Hull
Designer, Annie Kelly
Musical Direction, Richard Kilgour

The play was subsequently presented in Southwark Cathedral, from 22nd April 2010, by a 150-strong community cast working with a professional cast and crew.

JESUS, Merryn Owen
SATAN, Daniel Copeland
THE GOOSE, Michelle Watson
JOHN CROW, Charlie Folorunsho
JOHN TAYLOR, Kai Simmons
MOLL CUTPURSE, Caroline Garland
YAHWEH, David Meyer, John Constable
CROMWELL, Oliver Langdon
BEELZEBUB, Simon Jermond

Director, Sarah-Davey Hull
Designer, Annie Kelly
Musical Direction, Simon Jermond, Thomas Baker

The Players

ACTORS

WHORES

WATERMEN

JOHN TAYLOR

MOLL CUTPURSE

JOHN CROW

UNDERGROUND TUNNELLERS

CHERUB

THE DEVIL'S BAND

THE GOOSE

SATAN

YAHWEH

THE CHILD MARGARET

THE CHILD MICHAEL

CROMWELL

PURITAN SOLDIERS

BISHOP OF WINCHESTER

WILL SHAGSPUR

JESUS

BEELZEBUB

SEVEN DEVILS

PETER

MARTHA

GEORGE

THE SISTERS OF REDCROSS

THE NAVIGATOR

SURGEONS

NURSES

OSIRIS

ISIS

THOTH

THE SICK AND INFIRM

MARY SEACOLE

OLD TED

JUDAS

LAZARUS

THE CONSTABLE

HARRY BAILLY

FAITH

CHARITY

GEFFREY CHAUCER

CHARLES DICKENS

MARY MOTHER

THE MINISTER

THE BISHOP

THE BODY OF CHRIST

THE LOST SOULS

DEVIL GUARD

ANGELS

The stage directions indicate the preferred locations for
a production on Bankside, beginning at Shakespeare's
Globe and ending at Southwark Cathedral. The Cycle can
be adapted to any performance environment.

THE CREATIONS AND FALL

Prologue: The Goose At Liberty

*The Globe Theatre, Southwark. The backcloth is a huge map of Bankside, surmounted by curtains depicting the Heavens. The punters are ushered into a "new medieval" carnival atmosphere by ad libbing ACTORS, WHORES and WATERMEN (ferrymen). PLAYERS sing **The Ballad of Mary Overie**. JOHN TAYLOR, the "Water Poet", mingles with the crowd, clutching an oar, improvising a running commentary on the relevant verses of the Ballad.*

TAYLOR: Mary Overie, your patron saint of Actors, Whores and Watermen… Mary the ferryman's daughter – her Old Man owned half Bankside – and what an old miser! Puts it about that he's dead, right? So his family'll fast, out of respect – save him the price of feedin' 'em. Only he can't resist sneaking back, can he? See how they're gettin' on with their mournin'. Only they're not, are they? They're having a rave! Old Man Overie comes bustin' in on 'em. Only what's he forgotten? He's supposed to be six feet under. They think it's the Devil himself. One of 'em grabs an oar, bashes his brains out. No more resurrections for him! Mary's young man hears the news – he's in such a hurry to marry her and claim her inheritance – gallopin' up Maiden Lane, gets thrown off his horse. Another dead! She's gone and lost her husband-to-be and her Old Man – twice! A sign from God.

The Ballad ends. JOHN TAYLOR comes up on stage. He bangs his oar for silence, working the punters like a fairground barker.

Row up, row up, for The Southwark Mysteries.
As revealed to mad John Crow,
Who did walk The Goose at Liberty.
They say he walked her up from Crossbones
To the dock of Mary Overie.
Now don't take that as Gospel, mind.
It's more your oral history…

MOLL CUTPURSE, the "Roaring Girl of Bankside", comes up on stage, in Jacobean male drag with britches and a pipe, interrupting him.

MOLL: Woah, John boy! Woah, John Taylor! Woah!

TAYLOR: Would you Adam and Eve it? Seven lines into my Prologue, and here's Moll Cutpurse, that notorious Bankside baggage, sticking her big oar in.

MOLL: Don't get the hump, John Taylor boy. Let's hear it for our very own Bankside Bard, your actual Thames ferryman, the man who put the dog in doggerel, ladies and gentlemen, Mister John Taylor!

MOLL orchestrates the audience's applause, effectively ending JOHN TAYLOR's prologue.

Coming up, we've got John Crow, your original Whore's Prophet, here to conjure up The Goose at Liberty. 'Ere... Tell you what, John Taylor, these "Mysteries"... They're a bit... phwoar! Eh, John? Bit Sarf London.

TAYLOR: Well... They're your *Southwark* Mysteries, innit? Your *Oral* history. "Where your Actors and Whores are your Keepers of Doors what open into The Liberty." Your secret hermetical knowledge, what was revealed by The Goose to John Crow in his vision.

MOLL: Yeah... John Crow reckons Mary Overie founded her nunnery on the site of the old Temple of Isis...

MOLL points out Southwark Cathedral on the map.

Church of St Mary Overie. What is now your Southwark Cathedral.

TAYLOR: Overie, as in "over the river"...

MOLL: Over 'ere!

JOHN TAYLOR uses his oar to indicate The Liberty and the Clink Prison on the map.

TAYLOR: The Liberty of the Clink. Took its name from the old Clink Prison – 'ere. Now, The Liberty is outside the law of the City of London. See, over there, the City Fathers rule with a rod of iron. No drinking. No baiting the bear. No whoring...

MOLL: And no acting! Whereas Over 'ere – taverns, bear-pits, theatres, "stews" – your brothels... You got your Whores licensed by the Bishop of Winchester...

TAYLOR: Your Winchester Geese. Disportin' themselves, they was, bare-breasted on Bankside! We used to make a pretty penny ferrying Gents over from the City. Then the bloody Puritans go and close the theatres.

MOLL: Woah! Woah! Woah! These Geese. If they was licensed by the Bishop, how come they was buried in unconsecrated ground?

TAYLOR: Ah, yes! The Church has a few questions to answer... The old Crossbones Graveyard, your "Magdalene's" or "Single Women's" Burial Ground. Your charnel pit for paupers and prostitutes. That same Crossbones Graveyard what was of late disturbed by work on the Jubilee Line Extension.

He points at Crossbones, marked with crosses and skulls at the heart of the map.

MOLL: John Crow says they dug up The Goose's bones.

TAYLOR: Thereby setting in motion a train of infernal consequences what are now come to pass, as you shall see. As revealed to mad John Crow, who did walk The Goose at Liberty.

They present JOHN CROW, a ragged street-shaman, staring fixedly, in trance. Enter the JUBILEE LINE TUNNELLERS, construction workers in hard-hats and fluorescent jackets, wielding shovels and pickaxes, marching and chanting to a clanking rhythmic beat.

TUNNELLERS: O deep in the bowels of Borough mud
    We dig and we delve eternally.
    By the skin of our teeth, by the sweat of our blood,
    To build the Extension to Jubilee.

    O the earth is fetid and the air is foul.
    We'll be breaking this rock till Judgement Day.

FOREMAN: Yet you never will see a tunneller scowl.

ALL: Why should we? We're all on double pay.

1ˢᵗ TUNNELLER: Jesus! This place gives me the creeps.

2ⁿᵈ TUNNELLER: The workers are getting restless, Boss.

ALL: They say that the Devil himself here sleeps,
    In this unhallowed boneyard down under Redcross.

FOREMAN: Come on you boneheads, just one more bash.
    Our backs to the task we must bend us.
    Let us pile-drive this pit. One! Two! Three and –

They raise their tools to strike at the heart of the map. Trumpet blast. They freeze.

1ˢᵗ TUNNELLER: What is it?

FOREMAN: O Heaven defend us!

Trumpet blast. The map rips open. Enter, through the tear, an infernal procession: a ghastly CHERUB blowing a trumpet; a band of DEVILS playing a danse macabre; THE GOOSE, a feisty medieval whore. The DEVIL'S BAND segues into her song from **The Book of The Goose**.

GOOSE: I was born a Goose of Southwark
    By the Grace of Mary Overie,
    Whose Bishop gives me licence
    To sin within The Liberty.
    In Bankside stews and taverns
    You can hear me honk right daintily,
    As I unlock the hidden door,
    Unveil the Secret History.

I will dunk you in the river
And then reveal my Mystery.

JOHN CROW kneels before her.

'Ello, John! Fancy a dunk?

*JOHN CROW and THE GOOSE sing **John Crow's Riddle**.
The PLAYERS join in on a rousing chorus.*

CROW: John Crow with a riddle in a madcap rhyme,
    Here to reveal My Mystery,
    In London Town at the End of Time,
    John he go down on History.

GOOSE: For tonight in Hell they are tolling the bell
    For the Whore that lay at the Tabard.
    And well we know how the carrion crow
    Doth feast in our Crossbones Graveyard.

PLAYERS: With a hey ho jolly Jack Crow
    And his merry merry band of outlaws O
    Never stumble when he trips
    Mad clown of the Apocapocapocapocapocapocapoca...

*They babble, stuck on the word. Infernal cacophony. Enter
SATAN, a pantomime Devil with horns, tail and pitchfork. Exit
PLAYERS in confusion and terror.*

SATAN: Aaaaaaand... Cut!

*THE GOOSE, JOHN CROW, MOLL CUTPURSE and
JOHN TAYLOR remain frozen where they stand, entranced.*

Satan and Yahweh

The ghastly CHERUB blows his trumpet. The celestial curtains open to reveal YAHWEH, the archetypal Old Man with the White Beard, seemingly oblivious to the mayhem down below.

YAHWEH: I am gracious and great, God without a beginning,
    I am maker unmade, all might is in me.
    I am life and the way unto wealth-winning.
    I am foremost and first, as I bid shall it be…

    *He stops, gazing down aghast, as SATAN interrupts him, addressing
    the punters directly.*

SATAN: Methinks you all know who I am.
    Methinks you know me well.
    Methinks we can do business
    For you all have souls to sell.
    And some of you have contracts signed
    And sealed, your shares in Hell.

    Methinks you know my Moral Tale.
    You know the parts I play
    From Man's first fumbling Fall from Grace
    To his Last Judgement Day,
    When some forever in my debt
    Will have all Hell to pay.

    Methinks you've heard the rumours
    How now I do conspire
    To fritter Man and all his Works
    In everlasting fire.
    To tell the Truth… (*Sniggers.*) but how can I?
    I'm a compulsive Liar.

YAHWEH: Satan!

SATAN: You called?

YAHWEH: I thought I had consigned thee to the Pit.

SATAN: Ah, so you did – nor am I out of it,
    Befouled, besmirched, besmeared and all beshitt!

YAHWEH: Devil! Why torment these simple souls?

SATAN: Why, but to trap and trick 'em.

YAHWEH: I have books, with lists of thy bestial acts...

SATAN: You know where you can stick 'em!
    When I behold the blood with which
    Your Christian Name is tainted,
    It occurs to me I may not be
    As black as I am painted.
    So, before the Worm turns,
    Before London burns
    And the Thames River bubbles and boils,
    And the Seventh Seal is broken,
    And the graves yawn open,
    What say we agree the division of spoils?

YAHWEH: You ask me to bargain for the souls of Men?

SATAN: Me and you, Godfather, we're in this together.
    When these here souls crawl out of their holes...

YAHWEH: Each soul in its State shall be fixed forever.

SATAN: So... Here's the pitch.
    You take the north bank.
    All your God-fearing souls, your Men of the City.
    Gimme the Heretic, the Whore, the outcast, the outlaw,
    And the Bishop that licensed their Southwark Liberty.

YAHWEH: Each Man by his works alone must be judged.

SATAN: Yah!
    And we know how the Letter of the Law may be smudged.
    But wait! My best jest!
    My most haggardy Whore
    Like a bat out of Hell is of late broken loose.
    In the Bankside Liberty, they whisper her Heresy.
    Her Crow Prophet calls her The Winchester Goose.

He snaps THE GOOSE and JOHN CROW out of their trance.
They reanimate.

YAHWEH: Devil, do you dare to raise the Dead
    Before their Doomsday and the Last Trump sound?

GOOSE: No use blamin' 'im, mate.
    You got a complaint – talk to London Underground.

YAHWEH seems dumbfounded. SATAN guffaws.

YAHWEH: Without my Command, the Great Whore
    is loosed?

GOOSE: Got it in one, dear. Looks like your Roast is Goosed.

SATAN: Watch your tongue, Woman. Take it from me,
    When talking to God, it's as well to use tact.

GOOSE: You old hoofers don't frighten me.
    (*Aside.*) They're such a predictable Double Act.
    Now pipe down, the pair of you,
    Don't get ideas below your Station.
    What are you? Two bit-players
    In my Bankside Revelation.

THE GOOSE emphasises her point, poking SATAN, who backs
off, though evidently relishing her brazen cheek.

YAHWEH clears his throat.

YAHWEH: Would it be too much to ask that we stick to
    the script?

THE GOOSE and JOHN CROW exchange nonplussed looks.
JOHN TAYLOR, and MOLL CUTPURSE wake, rubbing
their eyes.

Mystery Plays? Creation? Adam and Eve? When I was
offered the part of God, I was given to understand it
was the lead. "I am gracious and great, God without a
beginning..."

TAYLOR: No offence, er... Lord, but you're talkin' your medieval Mysteries, yeah? Your York Cycle. These are your *Southwark* Mysteries.

YAHWEH: Song and dance routines with old slappers? I suppose it's too much to hope that my Son gets so much as a walk-on.

CROW: *Your* Son? Nah! Respect and honour to Brother Man Jesus, and if he cares to put in an appearance we'll do our best to make him feel at home. But he's no Son of *yours*!

YAHWEH splutters in disbelief. SATAN guffaws.

No, you're the false god. It was only after the Divine Female got banged up in the material universe, that she give birth to you. You? The True God? I don't think so!

YAHWEH: I am the One, the *Only*...

CROW: Then how come you're always at war with your Shadow?

JOHN CROW indicates SATAN, who roars with laughter. YAHWEH makes a supreme effort to control his rage.

SATAN: Gimme Six Six Six!
Gimme Nine Nine Nine!
Gimme Goose! Gimme Crow!
Gimme! Gimme what is mine!

YAHWEH: Hark! The Voice of the Serpent in Eden.

CROW: O, we know All About Eve
And how she got ambushed.

GOOSE: How I fell to earth
And fell in among the Heathen.

CROW: Question is: did she fall?

GOOSE: Or was I pushed?

The Creations

The BAND plays enchanted music. Enter MARGARET and MICHAEL, two contemporary streetwise children, born and raised in a travelling theatre company. MICHAEL carries an apple. MARGARET is dressed as a teacher with a mortarboard and cane. She teases SATAN, who retreats, observing from a safe distance, evidently afraid of her. A bell chimes. Tableau: MICHAEL holds up the apple; MARGARET plays teacher, flexing the cane.

MICHAEL: Here is a box of sweets,
   Not to be eaten.

MARGARET: Here the hungry child, some say
   Deserves to be beaten.

The bell chimes. JOHN CROW performs a ritual purification, swigging from a bottle and spitting a fine spray about the stage. MARGARET and MICHAEL drop out of character, addressing the punters as themselves.

MARGARET: I mean, what kind of God wants to keep Knowledge to himself? What if that was the Devil, and the Real God was in Adam and Eve, only they fell asleep?

MICHAEL: The Big Sleep! Like the Devil tells them he's the only God and they have to worship him and...

MARGARET: And Eve she's like "Adam, wake up!" Because she's already eaten the apple, yeah? – from the Tree of Knowledge. Which is what the Real God wants her to do – wake up! Which is why he sent the Serpent. Or should I say "S/He" – 'cuz before God becomes male and female, S/He's like everything and nothing, with no way of knowing what's what, right? What if Eve is like God's way of checking it out?

MICHAEL: John Crow says she's like the Goddess who reaches for the Light and takes a dive into Darkness and Chaos. Splat! Mind into matter.

MARGARET: He says evolution is the story of her trying to wake up.

Bells chime. JOHN CROW makes ritual passes, prostrates himself. YAHWEH, on high, mutters in disbelief.

YAHWEH: That's right, bring out the chicken feathers! Corrupt your children! Before you know it you'll be sacrificing them on some pagan altar!

CROW: No, that's you! Abraham and Isaac? We're still on the Creations.

The PLAYERS form a CHORUS, intoning a sustained "O" sound similar in resonance to the Hindu-Buddhist OM, filling the theatre with a mantric drone. MARGARET and MICHAEL speak in unison as the CHILD.

CHILD: In the beginning… what God was, God only know. For there was nothing what God wasn't.

CHORUS: As above, so below.

CHILD: All was One and the One was in the O. Don't ask us what that means. Ask John Crow.

CROW: Before Time was, in Eternity…

CHORUS: John Crow walk The Goose at Liberty.

CROW: When God the Father No more than twinkle in he Mother eye.

CHORUS: Goose in the Sky.

CROW: When old Satan No more than tremor in old Yahweh sleep.

CHORUS: Goose in the Deep.

GOOSE: When all was One, Within, without, as above, so below.

CHORUS: Goose in the O… Goose in the O… Goose in the…
OOOOOOOOOOOOOOOOOOOOOOOOOOOOOOOOO
IIIIIIIIIIIIIIIIIIIIIIIIIIIIIIIIIIIIIIIIIIIIIIIII
AAAAAAAAAAAAAAAAAA
MMMMMMM

A gong sounds and fades. The drone persists. The CHORUS forms the Voice of the One God, chanting the IAMs. THE GOOSE, the CHILD (MARGARET and MICHAEL), YAHWEH, SATAN and JOHN CROW express aspects of the Godhead.

GOOSE: In the beginning, unbegun IAM

CHILD: Mother of God and unbegotten Son IAM

GOOSE: Before the Word made Flesh, in the One IAM

CHORUS: As above so below IAM

GOOSE: Before the God made Man, in the O IAM

YAHWEH: All Knowing

SATAN: But there's Nothing else to Know IAM

CHILD: In God and Man, the uncreated Mind IAM

CROW: Unconditioned, unconfigured, unconfined IAM

CHORUS: As above so below IAM

GOOSE: Before the Man made God in thought to know IAM

YAHWEH: All Mighty

SATAN: But there's Nowhere else to go IAM

CROW: In the one hand clapping, the sound IAM

GOOSE: That which must be lost for to be found IAM

YAHWEH: That I am

SATAN: Then what am I, when I'm around?

GOOSE: Casting my reflection on the deep IAM

CROW: Struggling to rouse I self from sleep IAM

The CHILD breaks the rhythm.

CHILD: God sez: gee, gets kinda lonely
    Alone in this night of glittering stumps of carbon.
    God sez: let's try it another way,
    Let's see what happen when carbon decay.
    God tell the Mother S/He never knowed: "Bye, Ma."
    God set out on a journey.
    So on that fateful Day of his free-willed choosing…
    God set out to find the very thing S/He keep losing.

Drumming. Creation dance. Rhythmic chant.

YAHWEH: Naked Singularity, Big Bang IAM

SATAN: In Nature red and raw in Serpent fang IAM

YAHWEH: In the Word as in the syllable seed IAM

SATAN: In genetic code now cracked Now Read IAM

CROW: In Trance, as without, so within IAM

GOOSE: In the Dance, Siva-Sakti, free from Sin IAM.

CROW: In Adam and Eve as in the Snake IAM

GOOSE: When Eve bite the Apple wide Awake IAM

CROW: God say: this little moisten clay… This rogue strip of…

CHORUS: D… N… A…

GOOSE: Is where I come to play.

Exit MARGARET and MICHAEL, playing.

JOHN CROW takes centre stage, possessed by a manic energy, swigging from a can of beer, doing his "drunk" routine.

CROW: Man say: shurely shome mishtake
    Mushta been that bastard snake
    Done bit me in the heel
    Or why elshe do I feel
    So abandon and forshake.

YAHWEH: A curse upon the Woman
    Who did break My Holy Law.

CROW: The Spirit trapped in flesh,
    In the body of a Whore?
    O, but there's a twist.
    Her True Love will not forsake her.
    He will come to heal the rift,
    With a kiss to awake her.
    To heal the Wounds of Time
    In a Vision of Eternity.

YAHWEH: O, my Son will come, John Crow.
    I shall send him to judge thee.

The MUSICIANS play archaic break-beats under JOHN CROW's rap.

CROW: Kindred, cut to the chase.
    Ho! Let's get this mule kickin'!
    Are we plump for the pluckin'?
    Are we ripe for the pickin'?
    'Cuz some ah dem god dem
    Want we stack like factory chicken.
    Dem have dem way, Judgement Day,
    Dem finger lickin'.

    But you know John Crow,
    Never do what he ought 'ter.
    Him say, False God, before you go
    Lock up your Daughter,
    Before you send your Son
    Like a lamb to the slaughter,
    'Fore you do we the Fire
    We go do you the Water!

YAHWEH: Let... him... be... struck... down!

YAHWEH points his finger. Explosion. YAHWEH disappears in a puff of smoke. The celestial curtains close. JOHN CROW staggers as if struck by lightning. SATAN chortles.

SATAN: God is dead, John Crow, my son.
    You owe me one.

The Fall

Banging on the doors of the theatre.

SOLDIER: In the name of the Lord Protector.

The doors burst open. CROMWELL and his PURITAN SOLDIERS march through the pit and onto the stage.

CROW: What the fuck's going on? Who the fuck are you?

CROMWELL: I am iron-clad Cromwell,
    The Wrath of God incarnate.
    Here to harrow Hell
    In the heretic and harlot.
    To cast this Whore into the Pit
    With her accursed nation.
    As it is written in God's Book of Revelation.

CROW: That Book was written by a man
    In blood and bile and spleen.
    God calls upon his Son John Crow
    To wipe his Daughter clean.

CROMWELL: Heretic! Thy Mysteries
    Blaspheme our Bible story.
    Where is Our God in Heaven?
    Where the Power and the Glory?
    Where is the Tree of Life
    And Woman's Great Transgression?

CROW: We have another tale to tell
    Of the soul that fell from Eden,
    Of that female part of God
    Who sought herself to know.

CROMWELL: That female part was cursed by God
    Thou wicked John Crow.

CROW: The God that did curse her
    Was in your image cast.

CROMWELL: Another word from you, Brother,
    And it shall be thy last!

GOOSE: Over me and my John Crow
    You have no authority.
    I call upon my Bishop
    As defender of my Liberty.

CROMWELL: Ha! Where is the Bishop who would own
    this Whore?

*CROMWELL seizes THE GOOSE by the hair, forcing her to
her knees. The medieval BISHOP OF WINCHESTER appears
through the rend in the map.*

BISHOP: Hold, sir! For shame!

THE GOOSE runs to kneel before him. The BISHOP blesses her.

GOOSE: Bishop…

BISHOP: Goose…

CROMWELL: Ha! Methinks it is a strange Divinity
    That with the stews has such affinity!

BISHOP: My God seeks to parlay
    With this world's imperfection,
    And there it is, this Goose enjoys
    Her Bishop's protection.
    Here is no Law but the Law of Winchester.

CROMWELL: Since you honour not God's Law
    Here is my Law of Westminster.

*CROMWELL makes to draw his sword. He is interrupted by the
sudden appearance of WILL SHAGSPUR, in full Elizabethan
dress.*

WILL: "Thou rascal beadle, hold thy bloody hand!
    Why dost thou lash that whore?
    Strip thine own back.
    Thou hotly lust'st to use her in that kind
    For which thou whip'st her."
    – Lear, Act four, Scene six.

GOOSE: Will!

WILL: The Winchester Goose! Well what do you know?
    (Surveys JOHN CROW) And who's this piece of Rough
    Trade?

GOOSE: O, another upstart Crow. Will, John. John, Will. My
    Master Willie.

MOLL: *(Aside to JOHN TAYLOR)* Will Shagspur? 'ad 'im and
    all, 'as she?

TAYLOR: Not necessarily. Symbolical, innit? She's your arty-
    typical Muse.

CROMWELL: Aye, the Actor and the Whore, for sure,
    Are natural bedfellows.
    Ye do but stoke Hell's Furnace
    As the poker and the bellows.
    Thus shall I purge these sluices and stews…

WILL: Cromwell, you clack-dish!

    CROMWELL draws his sword. SATAN hastens to intervene.

SATAN: Gentlemen! Gentlemen!
    Much as I delight in learned disputation,
    Methinks it now behoves us
    To review our situation.
    Ye all hail from divers ages,
    The centuries traversing.
    Bethink you not it strange
    That ye be standing here conversing?
    When all of you by rights should be
    A-mouldering in the tomb.

CROMWELL: Then... It must be...

SATAN: It is! It is! It is the Day of Doom.

SATAN cackles. Everyone freezes. Dead silence. The ghastly CHERUB steps forward, preparing to blow on his trumpet. A whisper passes around the PLAYERS.

COMPANY: He is come... He is come... He is come...

THE SECOND COMING

Mary Magdalene

The ghastly CHERUB blows his trumpet. The DEVIL'S BAND play sacred music. The PLAYERS break into song.

COMPANY: He is come... He is come...
　　He is come... He is come...

CROMWELL and his SOLDIERS kneel, declaiming in time to the PLAYERS' scratch choir:

CROMWELL: He is come in the Name of the Father,
　　The Spirit made Flesh in the Son.
　　He is come in Might and Dread
　　To judge the Living and the Dead.
　　Lord, let thy Will be done.

　　Let the Angel blow the Last Trumpet.
　　Let the Devil bang on his drum.
　　Let the Veil be rent.
　　Let Sinners repent.
　　Lord, let thy Kingdom come.

Enter JESUS on a bicycle, a rough sleeper, unnoticed by all. CROMWELL rises, looking wildly about him for a glimpse of the Saviour. Seeing JESUS, he kneels, offering his sword.

CROMWELL: Lord, we are here to settle a score
　　With this Daughter of Satan,
　　A Witch and a Whore
　　Who must be justly punished
　　Under Moses' Law,
　　And this we shall do.
　　We shall strip her and whip her
　　And thus we shall shrive her,
　　And strap her in the cucking stool
　　And duck her in the river,

Until she is dead –
May God her soul deliver! –
As we now deliver her to be judged by you.

CROMWELL forces THE GOOSE to her knees.

SATAN: What a fiendish trick! What a fix to be in!
If he spares her life, he's breaking the Law.
But if he declares that they must stone the Whore,
At one stroke he denies the Forgiveness of Sin.
He must be Judge and either way
"His Honour" cannot win.

THE GOOSE appeals to JESUS as Mary Magdalene.

GOOSE: As a cursed creature closeted in care,
And as a wretched wraith all wrapped in woe,
Of bliss was never bag so bare
As I that now to Hell must go,
As I that now to Hell must fare
For these great Sins they say I do,
Unless my Lord see fit to spare
And his great Mercy receive me to.
Mary Magdalene is my name
Now I am come to Christ Jesu...

CROMWELL: By God, the Woman has no shame!

JESUS: Cromwell, what has the Woman done to you?

GOOSE: Have mercy, Lord, and salve my Sin;
Son of Man, now wash me free.

CROMWELL: There was never woman of Adam's kin
So full of Sin in no country.
She has befouled by frith and fen,
And filched men's souls in London City.

GOOSE: Be thou my balm, Lord, or I burn.

CROMWELL: With fire-blacked fiends she is bound to be.

JESUS: Cromwell, what has she done to you?

CROMWELL: Master, she was caught in the very act
of adultery.

JESUS: Is she your wife?

CROMWELL: Heaven forbid!

JESUS: Then…

CROMWELL: What has it to do with me?
When I see my neighbour's wife living in Sin…

JESUS: Then you must look to your own.
Let him that is without Sin cast the first stone.

*CROMWELL vacillates, torn between his instinctive mistrust
of JESUS and respect for his scriptural credentials.*

CROMWELL: If I could but be sure
You are the Son of Man.
For all I know you could be another
John Crow charlatan.

JESUS: That's just it! You don't know.
Before this day is out,
Even iron-clad Cromwell
Shall be tempered with doubt.

*JESUS raps on CROMWELL's armour, making it ring.
CROMWELL abruptly turns, marching his SOLDIERS off.
SATAN shouts after them.*

SATAN: It's a fix! It's a fudge!
Someone call the Hanging Judge.
Where are those fiends?

Exorcism: Seven Devils

BEELZEBUB and SEVEN DEVILS, dressed as paparazzi, appear in the pit. BEELZEBUB leads their chant with a headline.

BEELZEBUB: Oi! "Son Of Man" Spotted In Love-Nest With Whore!

DEVILS: He...
Ain't there yet, but just wait till we're done.
Never let the Truth spoil a good story.
We are the Sons of The Sun. Ra! Ra! Ra!

The DEVILS swarm up on to the stage, making buzzing noises. BEELZEBUB wipes his hand on his arse, sniffs it, politely offers it to JESUS.

BEELZEBUB: Beelzebub, Lord of the Flies...

JESUS, sunk in prayer, ignores BEELZEBUB, who irritably swats the flies swarming round him.

Oi! Jesus. If you're the Son of God, yeah? – Let's see you turn these stones into bread. Heh heh! No flies on me, my son!

DEVILS shriek with laughter at BEELZEBUB's joke. JESUS, completely absorbed, begins performing a ritual exorcism.

Oi! Cut the abracadabra
Magical mystery routine.
What all of our readers are wanting to know is...

DEVILS: What the **** does it mean?

BEELZEBUB: Our readers are pleading
To know where it's leading.
So Fiends, go fetch 'em a frenzy worth feeding.

The DEVILS close around THE GOOSE, furiously clicking their phallic cameras.

DEVILS: Go on, darlin'! Get your tits out! Phwoar! Ra! Ra! Ra!

*The DEVILS hiss, pawing at THE GOOSE. She howls and
cackles like a madwoman.*

GOOSE: Goosey Goosey Gander
Whither do you wander?
With seven fiends a-gang-banging
In my Lady's chamber.
Mad Tom be flibbertigibbeted,
And what of Mad Maud
Whom seven foul fiends do defile and defraud.

*JESUS steps forward to touch her on the head, calming her.
He performs ritual passes of exorcism and healing, making his
own sign of power.*

JESUS: Let seven devils from her be flit.
For in my love she is bound and lit.
Foul fiends, I you conjure.
Flee now her bodily bower.
In my grace she shall ever flower.
Till Death do here to die.

DEVILS: Ow! Ow! Help! Harrow!

*BEELZEBUB and the SEVEN DEVILS flee in terror and
confusion.*

SATAN: For Hell's sake! If you want a job doing, you've got
to do it yourself. You wait!

Exit SATAN.

The Spirit in the Flesh

THE GOOSE/MAGDALENE collapses, sobbing.

JESUS: Woman. Why do you weep?

GOOSE: Because they have taken my Lord from me.

JESUS: Maudelyn... Mary... Do you not know me?

> *THE GOOSE/MAGDALENE looks up, her face clearing, as if seeing him for the first time, in wonderment.*

GOOSE: Are you the Master? O, Rabboni!

> *She makes to embrace him.*

JESUS: *Noli me tangere.*
    For in Spirit, out of Body,
    I am here the Living Christ,
    Not some corpse consigned to Calvary,
    Returned in love and light
    To reclaim my Bankside Liberty.
    Maudelyn, thou art the very
    Heart of my Revealing
    Here to play your secret part
    In this mutual act of Healing.

GOOSE: Lord, do not trifle... Do not torment me.
    How much longer
    For my sins must I repent me?
    I have waited for you here,
    Waited for all Eternity.

JESUS: And now I am come to consummate the Mystery.

GOOSE: Before you loose my tongue to speak,
    Be warned I have a history.
    Other Mysteries here took root
    In your Magdala in Overie.

> *The DEVIL'S BAND plays. THE GOOSE/MAGDALENE sings.*

I am the Spirit
In the flesh elemental,
The wounds of all Time
In my garments are sewn.
Here on Bankside I sing
My song penitential,
Waiting for my Lord to come ferry me home.

O look at me now, dear,
Fetched up in the baggage trade
In some God-forsaken outpost
Of not-so-Ancient Rome.
I'm the Oldest Trick in the Oldest Game,
The price that must be paid, dear,
Waiting for my Lord to come ferry me home.

Lord, I have waited
By the dock of Mary Overie,
Here in the Shadow
Of the Millennium Dome,
Lord, I have walked
The streets of Eternity,
Waiting for my Lord to come ferry me home.

During the last verse, PETER hurries in, clutching a large black book. Unable to locate the scene in his book, he becomes increasingly agitated. The song ends. THE GOOSE/ MAGDALENE holds JESUS' gaze. JOHN CROW watches them intently.

JESUS: Mary... Maudelyn... I have work to do. There's a man in Guy's Hospital, Old Ted, the night watch. By nightfall, they'll be bagging his body in the mortuary, back of the old Tabard...

GOOSE: My brother is dying!

CROW: Goose...

GOOSE: Stay out of this, Crow. Don't get side-tracked. Me and your Man, we go way, way back.

JESUS and JOHN CROW scrutinise one another. Awkward silence.

GOOSE: Er... Jesus, John...

JESUS: John Crow with the broken wing.

GOOSE: Well, what am I supposed to do? Get me to a nunnery?

JESUS: Look to your brother Lazarus.
Go. Comfort him and wait for me.

GOOSE: Don't make me wait too long, Lord,
Or your comfort comes too late for me.

JESUS: I said I will come. Do you doubt me?

GOOSE: I do not doubt your Love, nor your infinite Mercy,
But if Lazarus should die, there dies a part of me.

JESUS: Woman, did I not say your brother's life is safe with me?

She holds his gaze in a battle of wills, then yields, bows and hurries off. JESUS gives JOHN CROW a long, hard look. MOLL CUTPURSE takes JOHN TAYLOR aside, ad-lib:

MOLL: Phwoar! Eh, John Taylor boy? That old Mary Mag-Witch... Getting a bit saucy back there, eh? Bit shirty! Anyone'd think she'd 'ad Him an' all. I don't like her insinuendo. I mean, Will Shagspur is one thing, but... Him?

TAYLOR: Moll, Moll, Moll. What did I tell you? What did I say?

MOLL: It's symbolical. *(Beat)* Of what?

TAYLOR: Your mystical marriage, innit? Your sacred and profane. See, your Goose, Mary Magdalene, she's your arty-typical Sinner, right? Now, if Our Man's prepared to turn a blind eye to her little indiscretions, well, that's got to be good news for the likes of you, eh Moll Cutpurse?

The other PLAYERS hush them. PETER sidles over to JESUS, nervously clearing his throat.

PETER: Master.

JESUS: Peter! My Rock! How's tricks?

PETER: (*Takes JESUS aside.*) May I suggest, Lord, we stick to the script.

JESUS: Yes, good to have you on the Book! But have you bound and have you loosed as I instructed you? Have you gathered all my parts...

PETER: (*Coughs, pointedly consulting the book.*) Now... where are we?

The Unclean Spirit

SATAN flies down from above, crowing.

SATAN: Here we are! Here and now, boys! Here and now!
Here's Mad John Crow come home to roost!

*He cackles. Everyone ignores his melodramatic entrance, except
for JOHN CROW, who reacts, shuffling and shaking, in trance.
SATAN gives him a poke with his pitchfork. JOHN CROW
convulses. PETER finds the place in his book.*

PETER: Ah, yes! Mark, chapter 5... "a man with an unclean
spirit. Who had his dwelling among the tombs; and no
man could bind him, no, not with chains: Because that
he had often been bound with fetters and chains, and
the chains had been plucked asunder by him, and the
fetters broken in pieces..."

*SATAN makes JOHN CROW dance, working the punters like
a fairground barker.*

SATAN: Roll up! Roll up! Gentleman! Ladies!
And ye shall see what ye shall see.
This freak of nature
Flip-flopping here before ye
Was once proud John Crow,
Whore's Prophet of the Liberty,
The Chemical Shaman
Who did raise his Kundalini,
Doomed to thrash on a straw pallet
For all Eternity.

*JESUS and PETER ignore SATAN's antics. PETER
continues reading from the script.*

PETER: "Neither could any man tame him And always,
night and day, he was on the mudflats, and in the tombs,
cutting himself with stones..."

SATAN taunts JOHN CROW.

SATAN: What is it this time, John?
  Dimethyltryptamine?
  Do we beat a drum
  In the church of ketamine?
  Do we play Siva to some lysergic Sakti?
  Do we catch a fever and then fall into a taxi?

SATAN taunts JESUS.

  I mean, for you to save a good soul,
  It's a piece of piss.
  So here lies one well wicked!
  Let's see what you make of this.

PETER: "But when he saw Jesus afar off, he ran and
  worshipped him. And cried with a loud voice, and said,
  What have I to do with thee, Jesus, thou Son of the most
  high God? I adjure thee by God, that thou torment me
  not..."

*JESUS approaches JOHN CROW, making the ritual passes of
healing and exorcism. SATAN squats on the edge of the stage,
delighting in JOHN CROW's response.*

JESUS: John Crow... Do you know me?

CROW: Jesus Christ. The Nazarene.
  Why do you torment me?
  Go shepherd your own flock.

JESUS: What is your Sin, John,
  That cries out for forgiveness?

CROW: I know no Sin,
  Only flesh and its weakness.

SATAN: Pride!

JESUS: It is said you were struck down
  For your Heresy outspoken.

CROW: For a Man to be made whole,
  He first must be broken.

JESUS: Mind your tongue, John.
    The Devil can cite scripture.

CROW: No Devil am I,
    But John Crow Trickster,
    The Prophet of a Whore.
    I think you get the picture.
    Now get out of my dance, Man.
    Go do your own revealing.
    Got to work this trance
    For my Goose and her Healing.

JESUS: John, you can run,
    But you cannot hide from me.
    For I am within you,
    As you are within me.
    You cannot serve two Masters...

CROW: Then will I not serve any.
    John Crow was born to honour
    The One made Many.

PETER: "For he said unto him, Come out of the man, thou
    unclean spirit. And he asked him, What is thy name?
    And he answered, saying My name is Legion, for we
    are many..."

SATAN: (*Joining in with PETER, bellowing at JESUS.*) My
    name is Legion, for we are many! (*JESUS pointedly
    ignores him.*) Is he deaf? Was it something I said?
    Gadarenes!

SATAN conducts the refrain of the DEVILS.

DEVILS: My name is Legion, for we are many!

JESUS ignores them. SATAN pulls a face.

SATAN: Be like that then! No use pretending we don't
    exist! Come on, you swine! Can't hear you! "What is thy
    name?"

SATAN and DEVILS encourage audience participation, conducting the refrain.

DEVILS: My name is Legion, for we are many!

JESUS ignores them. SATAN puts a positive spin on the snub.

SATAN: Deaf and blind! We have systematically degraded the enemy's defences!

JOHN CROW rolls a cigarette, lights it. JESUS persists.

JESUS: I gave you my sign, John,
  Dead crow hung in a tree.
  That as the One made Many,
  So the Many must return to me.

SATAN: Methinks our unclean spirit's
  Not so easily outdriven.
  This wanton John Crow
  Doesn't want to be forgiven.

JESUS: Your every profanity
  Makes a wound to weep in me.

CROW: What's your problem, Man?
  I never asked you to save me.

JESUS: If not by me, John Crow, then who?

CROW: By my Goose. By the Grace of my Goddess of Mercy.

JESUS: Then, by *her* Grace, your soul must be shriven.

PETER: But Master, the fool has no faith in thee.

JESUS: By *her* faith alone is his Sin, for now, forgiven.

SATAN: That's not fair! You heard him. He doesn't want to be forgiven! You can't go round saving souls that don't want to be saved! That's cheating! You're not playing the game.

JESUS: I'm here to change the game.

SATAN: Where are those Scribes and Pharisees?
(*Cueing DEVILS.*) Who does he think he is?

DEVILS: This is blasphemy!
God alone can forgive the Sins of Humanity.

JESUS: Kindred, in your hearts,
Wherefore reason ye?
Whether it is easier to say,
Thy Sins are forgiven thee,
Or take up thy bed and walk?
But that you may see
That the Son of God has the power to heal
All Earthly Infirmity.
I conjure you, John Crow,
Take up your bed and follow me.

SATAN: He's not following though, is he? He's smoking
a roly! Or is it a spliffy? O pizzle and pillicock! If you
won't play by the rules, I'm not playing with you! Come
on, you scum-bags.

SATAN stomps off in disgust, pausing to rally his troops.

Look on the dark side. The Goose and the Crow have
infiltrated the enemy's command structure. Now all
we have to do is prime Judas and before you can
say Armageddon...

DEVILS: We'll be back!

*The DEVILS clear a path for SATAN through the crowd. The
DEVIL'S BAND follow, blowing raspberries. Silence. JESUS
holds JOHN CROW's gaze.*

JESUS: Now, John Crow, if you will excuse me,
There are other wounded souls in need of my Ministry.

*Exit JESUS, leading off PETER and the other PLAYERS.
JOHN CROW scurries after them.*

THE HOUSES OF HEALING

Healing The Dragon

DRUMMERS burst into the theatre, leading a procession of MUMMERS bearing the carcass of a giant dragon – its skin a map of Southwark and Bermondsey – attended by MARTHA and the SISTERS OF REDCROSS, nuns and nurses wearing white aprons adorned with the red cross.

MUMMERS perform **George and the Dragon Rap**, *accompanied by a stylised dumb-show in which ST GEORGE, with his sword, battle armour and red cross emblazoned on his tunic, progresses from Christian martyr, through dragon-killing crusader and icon of English nationalism, to repentance for the evil he has done.* **The Rap** *ends with GEORGE bloodied and weeping over the butchered dragon.*

MARTHA and the SISTERS OF REDCROSS take charge of the situation, instructing GEORGE in the arts of healing the dragon. MARGARET and MICHAEL assist in the ritual.

SISTERS: Poor boy's in shock.
    Martha took him in hand.
    Got him started on the swabs and the tourniquet.

MARGARET: Should've seen the mess!

SISTERS: Neckinger the jugular, spurting and
    Spilling down Newington Causeway.

MARTHA: Here, boys, come hulk it
    Home from the Slaughtering.
    Come block and tackle it back from the Dead —

SISTERS: From the Fields of St George
    To St Thomas a Watering.
    Here, boys, to slake the scorched Dragon head.

MARTHA: On, boys, splint and bandage
    Up Margaret's Hill.
    Unravel the riven, the rupture, the spine.

SISTERS: Up Borough High
    To Thomas and Guy.
    To balm the charred head in Thames river brine.

MARTHA: Margaret, speed
    To Thomas Apocathary.
    St John's Wort, spikenard, alembic of mercury –

SISTERS: Send to Shad and Savory –
    Cloves, cinnamon and caraway –
    Herb for his garret, his Poor Man's Infirmary.

MARGARET: And comfrey for her bruises.

MICHAEL: It's arnica you want.

MARGARET: Arnica's for bones! Comfrey's for bruises!

MARTHA: O, for heaven's sake! Margaret, get both.

MARGARET hurries off on her mission.

MARTHA: The balm, George, the ointment.
    Put on your Red Cross Apron, play Nursey –
    If she thrashes about, do your best to calm her.
    Don't be afraid what the other Knights may say
    As they waste away inside their rusty armour.

SISTERS: Here, in a cavern in Camberwell, let the
                     drip drop drip of water in a pail
    Lap and salve the dragon's rank and rancid –
                     still smouldering tail.

Smoke and steam as the SISTERS OF REDCROSS ritually heal the dragon, stroking it, splashing it with holy water and "smudging" it with smouldering sage-sticks. Others wash the blood from GEORGE. At the climax of the ritual, the dragon revives and is danced away. MARGARET returns, loudly protesting to a POLICE CONSTABLE.

MARGARET: George, Officer?
   He was nowhere near the scene of the crime.
   Alibi? Cast Iron. If anyone asks
   He was with Martha and me at the time.

MARTHA comes to MARGARET's aid.

MARTHA: George, dear?
   He's out in the Yard,
   Enjoyin' a pint and a draw
   With Meera and Moll and Dickens Park Doll
   And the girls from the twenty-third floor.

They lead the CONSTABLE off.

And out of the mist, the ghost of an old Irish NAVIGATOR.

NAVIGATOR: Funny thing is, we was invited. They wanted
   navigators to drain the marshes. See, in the old days,
   St George's Fields was one dirty great swamp. Take a
   look at the old maps – Dirty Lane, Bandyleg Walk. We
   drained that swamp. We built our hovels and churches,
   and the Protestant Mob came and burnt them down. So
   we had to hold our Masses in secret, like here in Kent
   Street – a filthy, rat-infested slum, but no less the House
   of God for that. Kent Street, Tabard Street it is now.
   Here we honoured God our own way, but always one
   ear open for that knock on the door. And it kept coming.
   The Mob would burn the Mass House, and any other
   Catholic property, and drag our Priests through the
   street, tear them limb from limb. St Thomas More, they
   nailed bits of him to the door of Charterhouse, stuck
   his head on a spike at Traitor's Gate. They say Meg, his
   daughter, she talked the guards into dropping the head
   into her apron, and so carried it away for Christian
   burial. That's how they treated our holy fathers. Mind
   you, the one time we had the upper hand, in the reign
   of good Queen Mary, we did the same to them. The faces
   and the rosettes may change, but it's all heads on spikes,
   all the same…

*The old NAVIGATOR shuffles off, helped by a SISTER
OF REDCROSS.*

The Temple of Isis

A bell chimes. SURGEONS and NURSES wheel in a bed bearing the body of OSIRIS, hooked up to a drip. SISTERS OF REDCROSS step forward to perform the roles of ISIS and THOTH, holding a jug. ISIS circles the bed, performing the rites of death and rebirth, her ritual passes punctuated by regular chimes of bells, beat of a drum, clicks of sticks. THE SISTERS OF REDCROSS chant.

SISTERS: OM MA RA PA JA NA DEE
    O Isis Ceridwen Ishtar Sakti
    LONDINI AD FANUM ISIDIS
    Isis Kwan Yin Hathor Kali
    LONDINI AD FANUM ISIDIS
    Blessed are the wombs that are fruitful
    Blessed are the wombs that are barren
    LONDINI AD FANUM ISIDIS
    In London At The Temple of Isis
    O Isis Mary Magdala in Overie...

JOHN CROW shuffles forward, in trance, calling out uncertainly.

CROW: Isis? (*Pause.*) Isis?

ISIS, absorbed in her ritual, does not react. The SISTERS OF REDCROSS transmit the Voice of ISIS in whispered, echoing chorus.

SISTERS: (*As Isis*) I'm not like your Sky Gods, hung up on their Image.
    It's like you meet some stranger, you get this weird flash...
    "Hey, didn't I see you at Rameses' birthday bash?"

    Give not my children bones, John.
    Take a little flesh to fashion.
    They Done Time with sticks and stones, John.
    Give them Healing and Compassion.

Give it when you get some wino
Whining for your spare change.
Give it when your woman tell you
She need space and time to rearrange.
Give it out like Ali in the Costcutter Store,
Open 24/7 to feed another 5000 more.
Give it to the Men At Work
With their chemicals hazardous.
Give it here in the tenderloin,
Some nowhere border town name Lazarus.

*THOTH pours oil from the jug into ISIS' outstretched
hands. She anoints the body of OSIRIS. THE SISTERS OF
REDCROSS transmit the Voice of ISIS.*

Here, Lord, I anoint
Your Body dismembered.
Let me bind you in my winding sheet.
Let me stitch you back together.

ISIS and THOTH disappear into the Inner Sanctum.

Thomas' and Guy's

*THE SISTERS OF REDCROSS usher in a procession of THE SICK and INFIRM, as in a medieval pilgrimage, attended by SURGEONS, NURSES and MARY SEACOLE in period dress. JOHN CROW and the SISTERS OF REDCROSS recite the prayer **By the Grace of Our Lady Mary Overie** from **The Book of The Goose**, segueing into these verses from **The Book of The Crow**.*

CROW/SISTERS: Them that hop, flit and flap, like birds in
a trap,
Them that crouch in a house of rats, fearfully,
In the feeble and frail, and the Nightingale
Who sang in the House of Liberty.
In the letting of blood in the Bermondsey mud,
In the leech in St Thomas infirmary,
In the dumb that talk and the Dead that walk
And keep the Night Watch in the Liberty.

Enter JESUS, followed by JOHN CROW, PETER, JOHN TAYLOR and MOLL CUTPURSE.

MOLL: Sir... If I might make so bold as to welcome you on
behalf of St Thomas' and Guy's Hospitals.

JESUS bows graciously. Seeing MARY SEACOLE, he goes to greet her like an old friend.

JESUS: Mary! Mary Seacole!

MARY SEACOLE laughs, hugging him. JOHN TAYLOR sidles up to MOLL, observing.

MARY: Wha' appenin', Jesus? Look at the state of you! Skin
and bone! You need feeding up, boy!

TAYLOR: Who's that then? Florence Nightingale?

MOLL: Mary Seacole, your 'black nightingale'. Born
Jamaica, but we claim her as a local girl. Florence wasn't
the only nightingale doing a spot of nursin' in the old
Crimea...

*The entire COMPANY hush them. MARY SEACOLE leads JESUS to OLD TED, the patient in a hospital bed, hooked up to a drip, coughing and wheezing. THE SISTERS OF REDCROSS whisper fragments of **BRITANNIA HOUSE with the HAZCHEM**. JESUS works on OLD TED, laying on hands in healing. THE SISTERS OF REDCROSS chant.*

SISTERS: And Lo!
Out of the old mouths the toothless drooling
Slack-jawed miracles of modern medicine...
Out of the mouths racked and riddled with sores
Cancers pincers out of the blind staring eyes...
Out of pain release and rebirth...
As out of the mouths of babes and sucklings
In Tommies and Guys.

OLD TED sits bolt upright, staring at JESUS in amazement:

OLD TED: Jesus! 'Kin 'ell! I must be dead.

JESUS: No, you're not dead. Not yet, Ted. A day's grace...

OLD TED coughs and wheezes. JESUS slaps him on the back. He stops coughing, pulls out the drip and jumps out of bed, tapping his chest, showing himself to the other SICK and INFIRM pilgrims, who gasp and cry in astonishment.

For Lo! There is a time for waking and healing
And a time for the closing of eyes.
And as, in each life, I am Light revealing,
In each death, a part of me darkens and dies.
And there in St Thomas' I work my miracles
As here in my Bermondsey Guy's.
In my Nightingales and my Mary Seacoles
Who mopped-up my blood in the mud of Crimea.
Thus I tirelessly labour in your long night's Ministry,
To restore mine own body to wholeness and health.
Verily, verily, I say unto thee,
Physician, heal thyself!
For God is not real until in Man he be grounded.
The Doctor cannot heal until he himself be wounded.

JESUS gets onto the bed.

Here I take on the Sins, the loss, the grief of the world, its amputees and malignant tumours... Its short... circuited... motor neurons... Don't be afraid...

He invites the bewildered SURGEONS to operate on him.

No anaesthetic. I have to feel Man's pain.

The SURGEONS operate on JESUS. He stifles a scream, struggling to speak through the pain.

The electric gold and silver scarlet crimson city lights are become a million shards and spikes and splinters of glass... They prick, they pierce, they penetrate, striate, scouring my lungs, my liver, my spleen, my muscles, my bones, my heart, my blood, spitting and spurting, internal bleeding, here, here, here... Eli, Eli, Lama Sabachthani...My God! My God, why have you forsaken me...

SURGEONS: What are we to do? As God's Physicians
We are sworn to prolong human life.
Yet here we're reduced to being Body Technicians.
No pill nor potion, nor the surgeon's knife
Can restore this poor wretch...

JESUS: In old Ted gone terminal with the death rattle
of his forty a night... Stephen, David, Damilola... All
the boys cut down in the passage to manhood, in The
Borough, The Elephant, Camberwell, Peckham... And
the ones who cut them down? Can we learn to forgive
even them, the frightened bully boys who live in fear
of themselves, afraid to love, the truly untouchable....
Or is that too black and white? The Gangster down the
Old Kent Road... Do anything for his dear old Mum.
Laid on a bus-trip for the kids with special needs. So
what's a couple of knee-cappings between friends? The
Asylum Road drug dealer putting three kids by different
mothers through school...

JESUS gets up from the operating table, grinning through his agony.

In your Births, Deaths and Marriages
I kith you I kin you.
I Christ Allah Buddha
Siva Sakti Kwan Yin you.
Unborn Undying I Am Within You.

The SURGEONS back off, confused and afraid

For God is not real,
Until in Man he be grounded.
The Doctor cannot heal
Until he himself is wounded.

JESUS moves among the SICK and INFIRM, laying on hands: a BLIND WOMEN sees; a LAME MAN walks, waving his crutches. At each miraculous healing, they all cry out in wonderment.

Judas Iscariot

A man comes out of the crowd up on to the stage. Everything stops.
He and JESUS stare at each other in silence.

JESUS: 'Kin 'ell! If it isn't Judas Iscariot.

JUDAS: You said for me to wait for you.

JESUS: True. We have a score to settle.
      How much was it, Brother Man?
      Thirty silver shekel.
      Thirty shekel for a human soul?
      Cheap at the price, if you ask me.

JUDAS: And for that crime
      I'm still doing Time
      Outlawed for all Eternity.
      Yet when all's said and done, I kept my word.

JESUS: True, Brother Man. I called. You heard.
      And, here you are… The one man even I can't save.
      Judas, my man, come to dance on my grave. 'kin' 'ell!

PETER: I'd advise you not to talk like that, Lord,
      It makes a bad impression.
      You don't expect the Son of God
      To use such an expression.

JESUS: What do you expect? Some Sunday-school God?
      All scrubbed and polished? Speaks ever so politely?
      Only I can't see why anyone would want to crucify such
      An inoffensive little god me.
      Can you?
      In the House of the Harlot
      Man must Master the language.
      You see a man bleeding,
      You bring a man a bandage.
      Who are you to judge
      What's between me and my man Judas.

JESUS kisses JUDAS, who looks petrified.

Lazarus

JOHN CROW confronts JESUS.

CROW What about The Goose, Man? You gave your word.
   She's waiting for you now at Cross Bones Yard.

JESUS: True. Her brother Lazarus has taken to his bed.
   If I am not there with him, he is dead.

JOHN CROW calls the others to follow them.

CROW: To Crossbones, lads, that place of mortal sin,
   For Lazarus and Mary Magdalene.

PETER and JUDAS intercept JESUS, remonstrating.

PETER: To Crossbones, Lord? What business have we
   there?

JUDAS: It's nothing but a graveyard and a stew.

PETER: The stink of death is in the filthy air.

JUDAS: I would not go there now if I were you.

JESUS: Boys, do you not hear a word I speak?
   Young Lazarus is fallen fast asleep.

PETER: But if he's sick, Lord, wouldn't it be best
   To let him sleep?

JUDAS: That's right. He needs his rest.

JESUS: Boys, did you not hear a word I said?
   Then I will spell it out. Lazarus is dead.

He briskly leads the way to Crossbones. They follow.

JUDAS: I have a sneaky feeling
   We've all been here before.
   He would move Heaven and Earth
   To please that Maudlin Whore!

PETER: Coward! You mock
   The living proof of His Mercy.

The Dead shall rise again.
They shall see His Father's face.

CROW: He is going to heal my Goose at Liberty.
You're safe with me, lads. I know this place.

JUDAS: The Master is mad, if you ask me.
He's leading us all on a wild goose chase.

They approach the gates of Crossbones Graveyard. THE GOOSE/MAGDALENE stands at the door to her brother's tomb, grief-stricken. Her sister MARTHA tries in vain to comfort her. JESUS calls out to them.

JESUS: Mary! Martha!

THE GOOSE/MAGDALENE pointedly turns away. MARTHA intercepts him.

MARTHA: Help us, Lord. Our hope is fled.
Our brother Lazarus is dead.
Said he needed the drugs to kill the fear.
He wouldn't have died if you'd been here.

JESUS: Martha, I come to end your pain.
Your brother shall rise and live again.

MARTHA: Lord, I know that he shall rise
When you, descending from the skies,
Shall look what doom you shall him give,
Then may he rise, then may he live.

JESUS: I warn you all, both man and wife,
That I am rising. I am Life.
And whoso truly trusts in me
That I ever was and ever shall be
One thing I shall unto him give
Though he be dead, yet shall he live.
Tell me, woman, trust you this?

MARTHA: If you say so, my Lord of bliss,
It must be so. I ask no proof,
For you have always told the truth.

JESUS: Then tell your sister Maudelyn
That I am come to end her pain.

MARTHA: (*To THE GOOSE.*) Sister, leave your mourning song,
The Lord is come to right all wrong.

GOOSE: O for God's sake!

JESUS: Mary...

GOOSE: You're too late!

JESUS: Mary... Maudelyn...

GOOSE: He wouldn't have died if you'd been here.

JESUS: Let me see him.

GOOSE: Which bit do you want to see? His body's rotting in some unmarked ditch in Crossbones, along with the rest of us. I don't even want to think about his soul.

JESUS: That body will rise.

GOOSE: That body will reek.
That body's been rotting best part of a week.

MARTHA intercedes.

MARTHA: The body is within, Lord.
Mary dug it up by dead of night,
Embalmed it and performed
The sacred rites of rebirth.
She washed it and oiled it
To kindle its light, Lord.

GOOSE: Calling on your name, Lord,
For what it's worth!

JESUS: Mary... I'm only doing it to...

GOOSE: You and your bloody tests! You're as bad as your Father!

THE GOOSE/MAGDALENE again turns her back on him.
JESUS weeps. He performs the ritual of raising the dead,
calling out.

JESUS: Lazarus, awake! Open your eyes.
Lazarus, awake! Lazarus, arise!

LAZARUS appears swaddled in dirty bandages, looking like a wormy Egyptian mummy. Everyone recoils from the smell, holding their noses.

MARTHA: He is a bit whiffy!

JESUS: Take and loose him foot and hand,
    And from his throat unbind the band,
    The winding sheet and shroud undo
    And let him loose, and let him go.

THE GOOSE/MAGDALENE and MARTHA removing the swaddling from LAZARUS.

JUDAS: Brother Man, to please this Whore,
    Will you unmake the Natural Law?
    Look to the Living. What was it you said?
    Let the Dead bury the Dead.

PETER: Judas, you know where the moral lies.
    You gave Our Lord to Death.
    From Death He did rise.
    And now He is come at the End of Days
    The Souls of the Dead in the Flesh to raise.

JUDAS: Are you not God of the Living?
    Then go, heal your sick.
    We can do without some
    Crow shaman's conjuring trick.
    I can think of nothing worse
    Than that carrion flesh should rise,
    Reeking and riddled
    With maggots, worms and flies.

GOOSE: Judas, open your eyes and see
    Him that was lost is returned to me.

JUDAS: God does all this to save some crack-head
    Brother of a Whore?

GOOSE: Deliver us from Death, Lord,
    We that are Down By Law.
    Give the secret knock, Lord,
    Open the Hidden Door.

Let us in, Lord, all of us
And them that are gone before.

*THE GOOSE/MAGDALENE weeps, petitioning. JESUS
comforts her.*

JESUS: Magdalene, here I show you
  How the rift is healed
  Here and now the Spirit
  In the flesh revealed.

JUDAS: I don't doubt Sister Mary sees
  Into your murkiest Mysteries.
  The rest of us just see a corpse.
  I say let nature take its course.

LAZARUS: I'm pleased to hear you're so
  Concerned about my health,
  But perhaps you will permit me
  To speak for myself,
  Before you reduce me to some
  Abstract metaphysical...
  Take it from me, Man,
  It's all too freaking visceral!

  Four days my soul did rot in hell
  Till my Lord called to me
  And raised again this mortal shell
  Behold and you shall see.
  There's none so strong of Adam's seed,
  No, none that shrinks and squirms,
  This flesh that you all work to feed
  Shall be the food for worms.
  Yes, I who was worms' grub,
  Your mirror shall I be,
  Look into it and blub
  For you all shall look like me.

  Under the earth you shall
  Then cower on your couch.
  The roof of your great hall
  Your naked nose shall touch.

With things that creep and crawl
There you shall kneel and crouch.
A rag shall be your pall,
A bone shall be your crutch.
The flames of Hell shall lick,
And fiends your eyes shall pick,
With pitchforks poke and prick...

MARTHA: I think we get the picture.
Brother, good to have you back.
Though I must say you look thinner.
But if you carry on like that
You'll put us off our dinner.
For Our Lord is come to raise the dead.
At least we should see he's well watered and fed.

The COMPANY cheers, making merry. The cheering fades as a police CONSTABLE takes the stage to make a public announcement.

CONSTABLE: Ladies and gentlemen,
We don't wish to spoil your fun
Or in these Works to cast a spanner.
We would merely ask
That what must needs be done,
Be done in a dignified manner.
These Scenes we have witnessed
Are frankly grotesque.
Some may even think them Satanic.
But in leaving the theatre
We would kindly request
You to keep calm. There's no need to panic.
Out there, you will see things
To worry your wits.
It cannot be too clearly stated
That rumours of this here
Apocalypse
Are grossly exaggerated.

THE CONSTABLE and STEWARDS oversee an orderly procession to the next station.

184

THE CRUCIFIXIONS

The Last Supper I

The Tabard Inn. A long table laid for supper. A DEVIL'S TRIO plays ambient jazz. The yard gradually fills with "new disciples" including THE SISTERS OF REDCROSS. JESUS chats ad lib with PETER and JUDAS. Enter HARRY BAILLY, presenting him with a tankard of ale.

HARRY: There you go, Jesus.
    That'll put hairs on your chest!
    Compliments of the Tabard,
    Your Southwark Pilgrim's Rest.

JESUS: Cheers, Harry Bailly.

Exit HARRY BAILLY. JESUS takes a swig, offers it to JUDAS, who shakes his head.

JUDAS: Mine's a Bloody Mary.

JESUS: Buy your own. You've got your thirty pence!

JUDAS holds his gaze, then sidles off to the bar.

PETER: You're not going to invite him? You know what happened the last time.

JESUS: You can't have a Last Supper without Judas.

PETER: I don't understand. You know he'll betray you…

JESUS: And you'll deny me, I know…
    Not once, but thrice before the cock… John Crow!

JOHN CROW steps from the shadows, clutching a beer can, evidently ill at ease. JESUS greets him effusively, introducing him to the Southwark sisters, FAITH and CHARITY.

John, this is Faith. You know her sister Charity, your check-out girl in Superdrug.

FAITH: Don't be fooled by the names. We Baptist family.

CHARITY: When it come to religion, Man, we had we bellyfull. Last thing we want right now is the end of the world.

JESUS offers his tankard to JOHN CROW, who refuses, awkwardly raising his own beer can in a mock toast. GEFFREY CHAUCER and WILL SHAGSPUR cavort into the courtyard, drunkenly singing the chorus from a Bedlamite ballad, heralding THE GOOSE/MAGDALENE's entrance.

Yet I will find Bonny Maud, Merry Mad Maud,
And seek what 'ere betides her,
And I will love beneath or above
The dirty earth that hides her.

THE GOOSE/MAGDALENE hugs and kisses JESUS. He stares at her like a man in love.

GOOSE: Sorry I'm late, darlin'.

WILL: Masters Geffrey Chaucer and Will Shagspur. We're with the Bride

GEFFREY: We've had the Bride! Did I ever tell you Lord, that it was in this very Tabard Inn, the night before we set out for Canterbury, that a certain Winchester Goose…

WILL: Shh!

JESUS glowers at them. They stop laughing, suddenly ashamed and afraid. WILL stutters and stammers.

No offence, Jesus. God knows! That is you know… There are more… things… in Heaven and Earth…

JESUS: You're forgiven. "I" knows, I need all the poets I can get. Where's Blake?

GEFFREY: Lambeth, last I heard of him.

JESUS: Lambeth… And I am with him.

JOHN TAYLOR and MOLL wait their turn.

TAYLOR: See? You don't have to put on airs and graces with 'im. You got your Son of Man, right? Well, this is your Son of Man in the Street. 'Ere, watch... 'ere, Jesus! Any room in your crew for a Water Poet?

PETER: John Taylor, Thames ferryman and scribbler of doggerel.

TAYLOR: I have verses in praise of the Waterman's craft,
Of three hundred and sixty ale-houses and more.
I once sailed the Thames on a paper raft
With naught but a herring on a stick for an oar.

JESUS: (*Laughs.*) John Taylor, you have but to knock on my door.

Emboldened by his success, MOLL presents herself.

MOLL: Alright, Jesus boy? Moll Cutpurse, first woman to perform on the English stage.

PETER: Why should he want some trollop all dragged up in male apparel?

MOLL: Well, Molly Boys play Juliet.
Why can't Moll play Romeo?
Yer blood, right Jesus? Cheers!

MOLL takes JESUS' tankard, takes a swig of ale. CHARLES DICKENS steps out of the shadows.

DICKENS: Not wishing to rain on God's parade, but what about me old man in Marshalsea Prison? What about the Mannings and the hangings down Horsemonger Lane? Old Bill Sikes rag-nosed in some rat-infested slum on Jacob's Island?

PETER: (*Furious.*) What the...

JESUS: (*Delighted.*) Dickens! I knew I could count on you, Charlie. You and Charity are in charge of my social inclusion unit.

Cheers as HARRY BAILLY ushers in MARTHA, bearing a steaming pot which she sets on the table. The DISCIPLES take bowls. MARTHA serves. PETER ushers them to their places. JESUS shouts instructions.

JESUS: Mary on my right hand, Goose of Honour. John Crow on my left...

JOHN CROW reluctantly takes his place at the head of the table, sullenly bowing to THE GOOSE/MAGDALENE. JESUS takes his place between them.

MARTHA: Last time we did it proper
With the Paschal Lamb,
But these days such offerings
Are strictly for the Heathen.
The last thing we want's
A bunch of outraged vegetarians.
So it's stuffed peppers, brown rice,
And fish stew for the fishatarians.

MOLL: O you got to do the lamb, girl,
Dressed and succulent as sweetmeat.
He's got to teach us what it means
When we eat his head and feet.
Say no more. Moll has it sorted,
With sauce and dressing –

WILL: What? Mutton dressed as lamb!

MOLL has whipped out her knife in a trice, making to go for WILL.

JESUS: Moll!

MOLL: Sorry, Jesus boy.

She stashes her knife in her britches, smiling sweetly. The DISCIPLES ad lib among themselves. When all are seated, JESUS pointedly offers JOHN CROW the tankard.

JESUS: John Crow, will you not drink of my cup?

CROW: Yea, Lord, I shall drink my fill.

JOHN CROW takes and drains the tankard in one, slams it down defiantly. The DISCIPLES cheer, applaud, bang on the table. HARRY BAILLY proposes a toast.

HARRY: Jesus you are welcome
　　To our Southwark hospitality,
　　We bring homage and tribute
　　To our Lord of the Liberty.

ALL: (*Raise their glasses.*) Lord of the Liberty!.

The DISCIPLES cheer, applaud, bang on the table.

JESUS: Thank you, Harry Bailly,
　　But I must tell you plainly,
　　It'll take more than your licence
　　To enter my Liberty.
　　Kindred, we are gathered here
　　In solemn mystic union.
　　Mine own Last Wake and Wedding Feast
　　Conjoined in this communion.
　　Now to each place on Earth
　　I am returned to do Healing,
　　And according to each State
　　Is the Form of my Revealing.
　　Here in Southwark I am rooted
　　In your Common Humanity,
　　In John Crow and his Goose
　　And their quest for True Divinity.
　　For my Light shines in them
　　Though its brightness may blind them.
　　Such souls must be lost
　　That the Spirit may find them.

DISCIPLES: Amen.

PETER: Wedding Feast? I thought this was supposed to be the Last Supper.

The DISCIPLES commence eating. PETER clears his throat.

PETER: Lord, I know your penchant
    For the publican and sinner,
    I've tried to understand the love
    You bear to your lost sheep.
    Yet I would not see your Paschal Feast
    Reduced to a dog's dinner…

JESUS: True, a Son of Man is judged
    By the company he keeps!
    But is it so strange that an outcast god
    Should feel so at ease with his own?
    For the first time in the best part of
    Two thousand years,
    I can say I am truly at home.

The DISCIPLES cheer, applaud, bang on the table. They freeze in a tableau.

Pontius Pilate I

Three figures appear on a balcony/platform. The BISHOP surveys the tableau below, lost in thought. The MINISTER, a politician in a pinstripe suit, washes his hands in a basin of water. CROMWELL fidgets impatiently.

MINISTER: Perhaps we're taking it too seriously. It is, after all, only a play.

CROMWELL: Only? Minister, do you not see the doubt and confusion sown by poets and players? Why do you think I closed the theatres?

MINISTER: I thought it had something to do with the Plague.

CROMWELL: The cause of Plague is Sin, and the cause of Sin is Plays.

Silence. The MINISTER continues washing his hands.

BISHOP: We don't want to be too hasty. The matter could be raised at the next Synod.

CROMWELL: The Synod? Bishop, if we don't act now, there won't be a next Synod, or a Church! I say we take the blasphemer at his word...

MINISTER: O for God's sake, Cromwell! The last thing we need is a martyr. It may be best to simply ignore him. This Apocalypse business will soon blow over.

CROMWELL: Ha! So then I suppose we all just... crawl back into our graves!

They glower at one another. Long silence. The MINISTER dries his hands on a towel.

MINISTER: I say we defer to the Bishop. You do, after all, have what one might term a proprietorial interest...

BISHOP: O, I wouldn't go as far as that. The Church has not yet officially recognised it as an authentic Second Coming.

CROMWELL: God forbid! These mystics and visionaries are a greater threat to the True Faith than all the atheists in Christendom.

MINISTER: I see Cromwell's point. Any man who claims a direct line to God...

BISHOP: And yet Our Lord claimed precisely that. And for precisely that he was crucified. And by whom?

CROMWELL: By the Jew!

BISHOP: By the Men of the Law. The Defenders of the True Faith as they, doubtless sincerely, believed themselves to be. The upstart blasphemer must be put to death to protect their Image of God.

CROMWELL: Are you seriously suggesting...

BISHOP: I am saying that I would not want to find myself cast as a Scribe and a Pharisee. The fact is, much of what he teaches is entirely orthodox.

CROMWELL: Orthodox?!

BISHOP: Well, for a Christian of, say, the first century AD. Forgiveness of Sins, "God is within us"...

MINISTER: Precisely. And, in a multi-faith society...

CROMWELL: Careful, Minister. Our Church has already abandoned most of its articles of Faith. If it is now to imply that Jesus Christ is but One God among Many...

BISHOP: Here I am inclined to agree with my Lord Protector. Naturally, these days, we no longer wage war on men of other faiths. But to expect us to embrace Allah or Buddha or... Isis? Kwan Yin?

MINISTER: And who or what is Siva-Sakti?

BISHOP: I honestly do not believe the Church is ready to condone such a radical revision of the Creed.

CROMWELL: Then we are agreed?

MINISTER: We agree that something must be done.

They freeze in a tableau.

The Last Supper II

The scene reanimates. The DISCIPLES eat and drink. JESUS holds forth. The mood is tense.

JESUS: You see my problem? No, that's just it! You don't see.
I've told you, God is within you. So why look at me?

PETER: Are you not the Living Christ?

JESUS: If not, I am wormy in the place of the skull.
And the Conquering Worm say –

CROW: – Urp! Pardon me.

JESUS: John, you know the story of my brightest angel Lucifer?

CROW: Yeah, I hear he does a pretty mean impression of your Father.

JESUS: Not Lust, but Pride, may be your one mortal sin.

CROW: You'd know about that, eh Brother Man? The "I am God" thing.

JESUS: To your Goose be true, John,
For of all my outlaw band,
She alone has the power to anoint.
Don't you think she's worth more
Than a one-night stand
In some clapped-out Astral clip-joint?

CROW: Then the question you must be
Itching for me to ask, sir,
Is when you're going to make an honest woman of her?

JESUS: Here and now. Tonight, John Crow, she shall enter the Bridal Chamber.

JESUS addresses the bemused DISCIPLES.

And this Sacred Marriage let no Man profane,
Though the carrion crow pick at my rags and bones.
This is the Teaching I give to the Magdalene.
This is the Act that atones.

FAITH: Lord, teach us how to love you as you love her.

JESUS: I've told you already, Faith. Love thy neighbour.

FAITH: Lord, who is my neighbour?

JESUS: Faith, do you not know?
Here is your neighbour, Faith, John Crow.

JESUS playfully introduces them, putting JOHN CROW in the parable.

Here's John Crow mugged on Tooley Street, back-side of London Bridge. Sprawled on the railings, bruised and bleeding, foaming at the mouth. Here comes the Bishop to the rescue... But no, Bishop has his hands full with his Winchester Geese. Walks on by without a second glance, cross the road, down the steps to Southwark Cathedral... Now here comes Charity. She'll remember John Crow. She smiled at him once when she checked him out in Superdrug, lifted Crow Spirit... But Charity is miles away. She has this recurring nightmare, some psycho lurking in the Elephant and Castle subway. One look at John Crow, blood and foam, tripped out of his skull, Care In The Community. Charity walks on by, down Borough High, down to the Elephant and Castle subway...

CHARITY: No way, man! I never pass him by!

FAITH: Chill out, sis. Is only a story.

JESUS: Here's John Crow puking, crawling in the gutter, some would say it's where he belongs. But who's this? It's Ali from Costcutters, and before you can say "In Sha'Allah" he's on his mobile phone and the paramedics are ferrying John Crow over to Guy's, where Mary Seacole is waiting to bandage him up

The DISCIPLES look perplexed.

MARTHA: Lord, what of your chaste Christian souls
Who kept faith with your commission?

JESUS: Are they sick?

MARTHA: Not that I know.

JESUS: Then why call the Physician?
    For as I am the Living God, I come to plumb
    a deeper Mystery.

JUDAS: God the plumber! Yes, he'll drag the depths,
    Dredge every sewer and cesspit of the soul.

JESUS: How else may the God in Man ever be made whole?

JUDAS: And the Devil take the Marthas
    Who have served you faithfully!
    No time for Martha,
    Too busy making eyes at Mary!

Shocked silence.

JESUS: Is that all you see, Brother?
    Then is your mind sick
    And dead to the Healing of her Mystery.
    For the Holy Spirit
    Was never so quick
    As here in My Goose at Liberty.
    Magdalene! Enlighten your brother Disciples.
    Open your blood-knot in Overie.

THE GOOSE/MAGDALENE rises to address JESUS.

GOOSE: Lord, I am thy Other Half,
    The soul that fell from Eden.
    Forgive thy Goose's cackling laugh.
    Too much time among the Heathen.
    And did we die, or find another way
    To give this Love a chance?
    Forgive me, Lord, for asking, but
    May I have this dance?

*The MUSICIANS strike up Arab or Oriental music. JESUS
takes off his shirt, performs a formal, ritual dance with THE
GOOSE/MAGDALENE. She sings verses from **The Book of
The Crow**.*

GOOSE: In the church pews and stews,
  They whisper the news
  The ghost of an old Goose's Heresy,
  That the Magdalene Whore
  A love-child bore
  To the dancing Lord of The Liberty.

  I was in that Magdalene Whore
  Who walked the streets of Bermondsey.
  I traded hard in every Yard
  To keep the Child at Liberty.

  Come Trickster, Shaman, Prophet and Fool
  Speaking in tongues of The Mystery.
  Let all men contend – but God defend
  The lineaments of My Liberty.

  Come snake and whistle and rattle and drum,
  Come open me Cavern in Jubilee,
  Come open me Tomb to crackle and boom,
  And let the Bells ring in The Liberty.

  Come Christian and Jew,
  Muslim, Buddhist, Hindu,
  Let each to His own True Divinity.
  Let even the blind,
  Material Mind
  Walk His own hallowed path in Liberty.

  And seek not to bind the Visions you find
  In naming the parts of The Mystery.
  In naming the part, don't miss the Heart,
  The Heart of My Holy Liberty.

  Though you trick me up as Virgin or Whore
  And make me debase right bestially,
  I am the Dancing Child, the Door
  That opens into Eternity.

Song ends. The DISCIPLES applaud and cheer. PETER and JUDAS are stony faced. JESUS goes into his own music-hall routine.

JESUS: Now I have heard it said that I am dead.
  But it's only an ugly rumour.

What's the matter? You think God didn't get
A taste for gallows humour.

*They all stare at him, shocked. He shudders and falls. THE
GOOSE/MAGDALENE and MARTHA catch him.*

GOOSE: Here, tie up the poor flayed Christ Shaman.
Strap him, bind him, stop him spilling his guts
All over the killing floor.

*The DISCIPLES clear the table, laying JESUS on it. THE
GOOSE/MAGDALENE smashes a pot of ointment. She anoints
JESUS, ritualistically, as a priestess.*

Here, Lord, I anoint
Your Body dismembered.
Let me bind you in my winding sheet.
Let me stitch you back together.

*PETER watches, with evident misgivings. JUDAS is openly
outraged.*

JUDAS: That oil was worth its weight in gold,
You silly, wanton whore,
That oil we could have sold,
And passed the proceeds to the poor.

JESUS: Judas. You're wasting your breath.
When I am gone, the poor remain.
She is anointing me for Death.

JUDAS: What? You want to die again?

*THE GOOSE /MAGDALENE cradles JESUS on the table.
She kisses him.*

PETER: Woman, no more! You profane the Divinity.

JESUS: Peter. The Sin is in thy thought, not in what she does
to me.

PETER: Were we not taught to fear
The works of the Female,
And to follow the path of chastity,
And that who so much as look
At a woman in lust,
In his heart committeth adultery?

JESUS: Yet the Male and the Female
    Must be made one
    In the Spirit, not the Letter, of my Law.
    Where the thought of Sin
    Finds no lodge within,
    The Body and the Act is pure.

CROW: And – just supposing – you have shagged her,
    Or for that matter, one of your male disciples,
    Does that make you any less the Son of Man?

JESUS: John, you squander your soul on trifles.
    As the One made many
    In my body parts dismembered,
    Tonight here in Southwark,
    I am hung drawn and quartered.
    Two thousand years
    My wounds have been bleeding.
    Mary here's the only one
    Who sees where this is leading.
    Before this night is done, one of you shall betray me.
    Shall it be you, John?

JOHN CROW says nothing.

    God must become Man
    To conquer his mortality.
    Into the very jaws of Death
    A God must journey.

JUDAS: For Christ's sake, Brother Man!
    This is insanity.
    Haven't you been crucified enough already?

CROW: Far be it from me to side
    With Brother Judas, Boss.
    But don't you think it's time
    You came down from your Cross?

PETER: Blasphemer! The Cross is the root of Christianity.

CROW: Is this your God? The God of Pain?

JESUS: A Wounded Divinity?
    You got a better suggestion, eh, John Crow?

CROW: O... Why not? The female O.
　　Mother of All. Magdala in Overie...

MOLL : "Not the Cross, but the O." Nice one, John Crow.

JESUS: You're just the man I need to hammer the nails in
　　me.

CROW: How many times must the Son of Man die
　　To appease his God Father of Guilt and Shame?

JESUS: For My Sake, John Crow! You think I don't know
　　How many are crucified – and in my name?
　　You think I don't hear the hate and the fear,
　　That howls for the end of the world and its doubt?
　　You think I don't feel all the wounds I must heal?
　　You think I don't clock that Time's running out?
　　You think I don't taste all your Toxic Waste?
　　You think I don't feel your pain?
　　You don't think, God knows, God must die for Man
　　That Man may rise again.

Enter HARRY BAILLY calling.

HARRY: Jesus! Jesus, your Mother's here.

Enter MARY MOTHER.

MOTHER: Where is he? O will you
　　Look of the state of him!
　　He's wandered the earth for you,
　　Mary Maudelyn.
　　Now he's found you I hope
　　You will take him in hand,
　　Tell my poor boy to come home.

GOOSE: I'm doing my best, Ma,
　　But you must understand,
　　Your boy has a mind of his own.

JESUS: Ma... It's Time...
　　You have to let go of me,
　　Your son must die in Time...
　　To arise in Eternity...

GOOSE: Love, do you think
 I want you to die for me?
 Does it not occur to you, love,
 That I may not need forgiving?
 Could we not consummate
 Our love in the living?

PETER: Master, these are the Temptations of Satan.
 I warned you before of these Player's tricks.
 Your Southwark Goose and her Upstart Crow
 Have been messing about with the script.
 Lord, would you give your life for the soul of this Lady?

JESUS: For her and for all the Lost Souls of my Liberty.

JUDAS: Lord, do not die for Man, let alone for love of
 Mary.

JESUS: Sez you. Yet this night, one of you shall betray me.

ALL: Not I, Lord. Nor I. Never. No, say it's not true.

TAYLOR: Cursed be the Man who even thought to betray
 you.

MOLL: If Moll should chance to meet him
 In some Bankside back-street.
 Take it from me, Brother,
 That Man is dead meat!

WILL: And when he is dead, I say let his soul roast!

DICKENS: That Man is truly lost!

FAITH: That Man is Toast!

PETER: Surely, Master, that Man cannot be me.

GEFFREY: *(Crows)* Kikuriku! Kikuriku!

ALL: Tell us, Master, who might that Man be?

 JUDAS bangs his purse on the table.

JUDAS: Stop playing games! You all know it's me.
 So this is my Hell, to betray you eternally.

JESUS: It is done.
>Now put your mouth where your money is.
>God Is Dead. Inform the Authorities.

>*Exit JUDAS. JESUS sinks back in THE GOOSE/ MAGDALENE's arms, near death, making a last effort to speak.*

JESUS: Be led by Mary, when I am dead.

PETER: Be led by a Woman, Lord? A Sinner? A… 'tart'?

JESUS: For she alone knew where my secret path led,
>Where I must be made whole in each of my parts.
>Peter, of my Church, I made you the Head,
>But it takes a Magdalene to open its Heart.

>*JESUS dies in GOOSE MAGDALENE's arms. MARY MOTHER collapses on the corpse, keening. THE SISTERS OF REDCROSS gather round them, grieving. The SEVEN PAPARAZZI DEVILS break cover, rushing the stage, cameras clicking and flashing. ALL freeze in a silent tableau. BEELZEBUB relishes the headline.*

BEELZEBUB: "God" Snapped In Pagan Orgy!

Pontius Pilate II

The scene reanimates. The BISHOP, the MINISTER and CROMWELL survey the tableau of The Last Supper, aghast.

CROMWELL: Well?

MINISTER: We could have him sectioned, keep him under sedation: some basket-case with a God complex.

BISHOP: He may well be in genuine need of healing.

A knock at the door. Enter a POLICE CONSTABLE.

CONSTABLE: Er, excuse me, Your Grace, but there's a Judas Iscariot wanting to see you. He says it won't wait.

CROMWELL instinctively makes to draw his sword. The MINISTER gently but firmly restrains him. The BISHOP gestures wearily. CONSTABLE ushers in JUDAS.

JUDAS: Gentlemen, a message from the Master.

MINISTER: Well?

JUDAS: God is Dead.

MINISTER: No offence, but that's hardly an original proposition!

JUDAS: God is Dead.

CROMWELL draws his sword, makes to strike JUDAS down. The BISHOP restrains him.

BISHOP: No! "Vengeance is mine, saith the Lord."

JUDAS: Him that hath ears to hear, let him hear.
God is dead that Man may rise again.

JUDAS hurls his thirty pieces of silver on the floor, leaves. A long silence.

MINISTER: Well, then, provided it is carried out as tastefully, preferably painlessly, as possible, I suggest we proceed with the crucifixion.

The Last Supper III

Pieta. THE GOOSE/MAGDALENE, cradles the lifeless body of JESUS. The DISCIPLES chant.

DISCIPLES: I am all the death and pain of two thousand
years and more.
The unidentified body washed up on the foreshore.
I am Abel slain by Cain, Esau cheated of his birthright.
I am Stephen Lawrence walking home. Footsteps in
the night.

So mock me, revile me, do your damndest to defile me,
Make me crawl my crooked mile to Calvary Hill,
With sticks, with stones, with bottles and bones.
I am the last man alone with his suicide pill.

I am the Paddy navvy come to drain St George's bogs.
The Windrush family reading the sign: "No Coloureds.
No Irish. No dogs."
Thalidomide, I teach my stumpy hands to open doors.
I am the child raped and murdered in the place of
dead souls.

So hang, draw and quarter me, lamb to the slaughter me,
Don't forget to water me before night falls,
With poles, with pikes, with ditches and dikes.
I am the battered bride who's always walking into walls.

I am the bartered Child in the Slave Mart of Babylon,
The woman who died in a burning house trying to save
her children.

Give me your hate, your rage, your Mob on the rampage,
Your riot on the front page of yesterday's news,
With fingers, with fists, with blades that switch.
I am the bare lightbulb twitching in a cellar full of shoes.

A bell clangs. HARRY BAILEY calls out.

HARRY: Time, gentlemen, please!

CROW: Here's Christ in the gents.
    He's down on his knees
    In the vomit and beer,
    Scrabbling to put back together
    The broken pieces of the mirror.

MARY and MARTHA cover JESUS with a white sheet marked with a bloody cross. THE SISTERS OF REDCROSS pay their respects and follow them off in procession.

SISTERS: Here lay your hearts, your flowers,
    Your Book of Hours,
    Your fingers, your thumbs,
    Your 'Miss You Mums'.
    Here hang your hopes, your dreams,
    Your Might Have Beens,
    Your locks, your keys, your Mysteries.

Enter THE CONSTABLE. He gestures for those still loitering to disperse.

CONSTABLE: Move along, now. There's nothing to see.

He looks under the sheet, then taps on the iron bed with his truncheon.

Time, gentlemen, please!

JESUS wakes, as a dosser. He scrambles out of bed and scurries off. THE CONSTABLE addresses the remaining punters.

The "place of the skull" is now a restricted area. Move along. Nothing to see... It's only an empty grave...

THE CONSTABLE, ad lib, supervises the orderly evacuation of the yard, directing the punters join the procession to Winchester Palace and the Cathedral.

Corpus Christi

Winchester Palace. In the pit of its foundations, a group of PLAYERS, identically swaddled in blood-stained bandages, form a collective BODY OF CHRIST on the cross. The BODY writhes in agony. The individual PARTS speak, in sequence, according to their position on the cross.

Here
crook'd
on the moss-pock'd cobble-cross
Christ so loved the World
and Her Whore
Soul
He
toll
His
Own
knell
and go
Harrowing Hell
only to make Her Whole.

The collective BODY OF CHRIST rises up on the cross, dancing.

BODY: He who sees but the God
In the Garden of Paradise
Sees not the Man
In whom he is Sacrificed.
He that sees but the Man
Hung on the Cross dying
Sees not the Serpent
On the Tree of Life writhing.
He who sees but the Serpent
In The House of Correction
Sees not The God of the Resurrection.

For only when all my parts are gathered
When Man is within me in Body and Soul
And beholds his own face
In the faces of kindred
Only then shall God be made whole.

Only when Time opens into Eternity,
When what is Without is revealed Within.
Only then will we solve the Mystery.
Only then can the dance begin.

The collective BODY OF CHRIST sinks back on the cross, convulses, then goes limp and still. The SISTERS OF REDCROSS chant the last verses from **The Book Of The Game***:*

SISTERS: O God, don't die
Without telling us why...
Why we struggle for breath.
God, free us from Death...
We go open the Cave,
Bring God back from the Grave...
We go oil God's Body.
We go kindle His flame...
We go lay Him on the bed.
We go shake, go wake Him up.
We go Raise Him From The Dead
We go Turn Every Trick in The Game
To balm and to heal his Wound, to reveal
The Human Face of The God With No Name.

The SEVEN paparazzi DEVILS rush out of the shadows, cameras clicking and flashing. BEELZEBUB struts about, spitting headlines.

BEELZEBUB: Man, 33, Nailed To Tree...
Golgotha – Result... "God Is Dead" – Official.

DEVILS with pitchforks swarm into the Pit, dismembering the remains of the collective BODY OF CHRIST. The blood-stained bandaged PLAYERS are driven out of the Pit and - along with the punters, past the corpse of Judas Iscariot, strung up from a lamp-post - into Cathedral Yard, where a host of LOST SOULS perform **The Book of The New South Bank***. The DEVILS herd the punters in through the West Door of Southwark Cathedral.*

APOCALYPSE

The Harrowing of Hell

THE DEVILS have occupied Southwark Cathedral. The LOST SOULS are driven in chains, weeping and wailing down the aisle. THE GOOSE and JOHN CROW are paraded on a cart. A DEVIL GUARD swaggers in, with a clipboard and brandishing a dismembered human arm.

GUARD: Anyone fancy an Earl of Sandwich?

Ad lib, surveying the audience for contemporary villains. DEVILS drive in PETER, CROMWELL and JUDAS, bound by a rope around their necks.

CROMWELL: There must be some mistake! Do you know who I am?

DEVIL GUARD: Well, crap my trap if it isn't Mister Cromwell! With our old friend St Peter and... 'Kin 'ell! If it isn't Judas Iscariot! Yah! Yah!

DEVIL GUARD prods them with the dismembered arm, driving them off.

MOLL CUTPURSE and JOHN TAYLOR are wheeled on in a cage.

MOLL: Phwoar! Bit steamy in 'ere, eh John boy? I suppose you're going to tell me it's symbolical? Eh, John Taylor? Eh, John? Only far as I can see, you and me, John, we're up Neckinger creek without a paddle. Up to our necks in it!

The GHASTLY CHERUB blows fart noises on his trumpet, heralding SATAN's triumphal entry. BEELZEBUB and DEVILS make obeisance.

BEELZEBUB: Your Excremency!

DEVILS: Master!

SATAN strides up on stage, playing Master of Ceremonies.

SATAN: Roll up! Roll up! All you dead meat
That did meddle and muddle
And mess with the Mysteries.

BEELZEBUB: I'm hungry!

SATAN: I'm starving!

BOTH: Let's see what's to eat!

DEVILS: We're hot to trot and to take a few Liberties.

SATAN: Now, when the bell tolls,
When the drums beat.
I don't want to hear you dogs
A-barkin' and a-bitchin'.

BEELZEBUB: It's too late to complain.

SATAN: If you can't stand the heat.

BOTH: Tough!

DEVILS: There's no way out of the Kitchen.

Amplified sound of the Gates of Hell slamming shut.

SATAN: Observe now this heretic
And his raddled Whore,
Now Doing Time for Eternity.

DEVILS: Let's prick 'em and poke 'em
And prod 'em and phwoar!
For each of their acts of harlotry.

*The DEVILS set about JOHN CROW and THE GOOSE/
MAGDALENE, poking and prodding them with their
pitchforks.*

SATAN: O I've got plenty more whores,
That I keep within doors,
A-tremblin' in fear of the poke of my prick.
O and plenty Rogue Priests –

LOST SOULS: Will our Pain never cease?

DEVILS: A-thrillin' to the chillin' of the flames that lick.

SATAN: The unwashed and unwed,
　　The crack-head and smack-head.

DEVILS: A-hippin' and a-hoppin' and a-gettin' their kick.

SATAN: O and bad girls and rude boys, hark!
　　They make such a sad noise.

DEVILS: Now they know how far they fell for Satan's trick!

They poke and prod the LOST SOULS, who weep and wail accordingly.

BEELZEBUB: Roll up! Roll up! It is time to let loose
　　The Star of this X-rated Live Show.

The DEVILS make obeisance to SATAN, who bows modestly.

SATAN: Your Great Beast shall now
　　Get to work on this Goose.
　　Beelzebub, bring me my red-hot dildo.

BEELZEBUB cackles in anticipation, presenting SATAN with an enormous red phallus. SATAN makes to perform on THE GOOSE/MAGDALENE, but is interrupted by banging at the Gates of Hell.

JESUS: Open up, you Prince of Pain and Fear,
　　These Iron Gates that hold your Prisoners here.

SATAN: What bastard boy now makes so bold
　　To interrupt my Goose gang-bang?

A DEVIL GUARD calls out from the Gate.

GUARD: It is the Jew that Judas sold,
　　The one what on the cross did hang.

SATAN: Ow! This tale in time is told.
　　He crosses us since Time began.
　　Go gag his gob and grab his gold
　　And get him gone with all his gang.

GUARD: Nay, nay, he will not wend!
   His face is fierce and fell!
   He shapes him now to shend
   Our very Gates of Hell.

More banging on the Gates of Hell.

JESUS: Open up, you Prince of Pride,
   Your Iron Gates that shut your Lord outside.

BEELZEBUB: O Hideous One, I hate to say
   This cursed Jew is Heaven sent.
   We know how Lazarus got away.
   To harrow Hell his will is bent.
   Think you that we yet mar him may
   And bar his way and his intent?
   If he now deprive us of our prey
   Who will deny our veil is rent?

SATAN: Clack-dish! He connives
   To frit you with a frown.
   Go take up clubs and knives
   And ding that dastard down.

More banging at the Gates of Hell.

JESUS: This stew shall you no longer stock.
   Open up!

SATAN: O, kiss my arse!

*The Gates burst open. Enter JESUS, unarmed, escorted only
by MICHAEL and MARGARET as Angels.*

BEELZEBUB: Ow! Harrow! Our Gates are brock,
   And burst are all our bands of brass!
   Lord Satan, he has loosed the lock.
   I fear we are undone. Alas!
   Satan defend us from this cock.
   His wrath is worse than ever it was.

SATAN: Quit cringing, you great clown.
   One more word and you are dead!
   Go! Ding that dastard down
   And clap him on the head.

SATAN demonstrates, whacking BEELZEBUB with the phallus.

BEELZEBUB: Clap him? Easier said than done.
Clap him yourself, if you're so sure.

BEELZEBUB snatches the phallus, whacking SATAN with it, then runs to hide in fear.

SATAN: Are we not Many? And he but One?

BEELZEBUB: He will us mar, though we be more.

SATAN: Then must I do what must be done
To ding him down and shut that door!
Come gear me up with bomb and gun
To drown the Earth in blood and gore.

SATAN advances, swaggering and menacing. JESUS comes through the crowd to confront him, unimpressed by his bluster.

SATAN: How now, *bel ami*, abide
With all your flaunt and fear
And tell to me this tide,
What Mastery seek you here?

JESUS: The Mastery of what is mine,
Wherein I limb from limb am torn.
You have no power these souls to pine.
Your death-knells clangs when I am born.
Here in your Clink they have all done time,
That they might repent and, in time, reform.
They were never given to thee and thine.
The veil is rent. Your power shorn.
Now in my Father's name
I am come, as once before,
To free all souls from pain
To dwell in mirth for evermore.

SATAN: Your father? Old Joe the carpenter,
Who chipped his block, his crust to win.
Let's not forget Mary, your poor old mother.
They're all you can call your kith and kin.
Tell me, who made you so mickle of might?

JESUS: Demon, dim you down your din.
    My Father dwells in Love and Light.
    He has no end nor yet begin.
    In human form I hid.
    I bound my Light in skin.
    Suspect you never did
    The God that dwelt within.

SATAN: Methinks we tread familiar turf.
    You've had your Adam and your Eve.
    And Lazarus too, for what he's worth,
    There's no one else has won reprieve.

SATAN indicates the punters.

    Behold the Wretched of the Earth
    Awash with lust and sloth and greed,
    This motley crew shall ne'er know mirth
    Who did flout your Law in word and deed.
    Who the hell do you think you are
    To say they shall not pay the Price?

JESUS: I am that God whipped red and raw
    To clear Man's debt by Sacrifice.

SATAN: Have at him, fiends, with tooth and claw!

BEELZEBUB: What pick a fight with Jesus Christ?
    Go pick your own!

JESUS: I come once more
    To lead these souls to Paradise.

SATAN: Look! These tunnellers who dug up
    The bones of your dead,
    Their souls sure are sullied
    With their blood-money.

JESUS: They had jobs to do
    And mouths to be fed.
    They risked life and limb
    To extend that Jubilee.
    All these are only in thrall to thee
    By dint of thy darkest delusion.
    When they look to the Light of my Liberty
    Death shall have no dominion.

JESUS makes a ritual gesture. The LOST SOULS are miraculously released from their chains. JOHN CROW and The GOOSE/MAGDALENE remain in bondage. JUDAS, PETER and CROMWELL shuffle forward, tethered by a rope around their necks.

SATAN: Yah! Not all! Look! Iron-clad Cromwell
In hardness of heart put your bitches to birch.
And Peter the Preacher he must burn in Hell
For the evil men do in the name of your Church.
Yah! And Judas the traitor your body did sell,
And in your hour of need left you in the lurch.

JESUS: Yet each by his light sought to serve me well
Then let each, by my light, his own soul search.
For Peter my church's Foundations laid,
That were then shored up by stout Cromwell.
And had Judas never yet me betrayed
I would not be here now to harrow your Hell.

JESUS makes his ritual gesture of release. The rope miraculously falls from their necks.

DEVILS: Ow! Harrow! Ow! Help!

SATAN: Silence, ye whelps!
This cur shall not skulk 'twixt us and our feast.
We'll have the slut and the slag at least.
And what about these closet queers?
I've got a parlour full of Priests
Taking each other from the rears.

JESUS: They too are from your Power released.
I look not at their parts but here... *(Touches his heart.)*
Where Angels wrestle with the Beast,
Where there is Love, there is no Fear.

SATAN: O no, I will not budge
From what Levi's Law permits –

JESUS: Who are you to judge
What they do with their bits?
But them that do wilfully destroy
Who abuse and exploit and corrupt and defile.

SATAN: The Bishop who buggered the altar boy?

JESUS: May well in a Hell of his own stew awhile.
    But not just to stew in his own rancid juice,
    But to repent and be reconciled,
    To repair the damage, and to heal the abuse,
    The scars he has left in the heart of the Child.
    For all that enter my keep
    Their bonds I can break,
    There is none here asleep
    That I cannot wake.

SATAN: Yah! You twisty-talk! You say the damned are blessed.
    There can be no mercy for The Bishop of Winchester.

DEVILS lead in the BISHOP OF WINCHESTER, hands bound, at pitchfork-point.

JESUS: Even Bishops may not from Judgement be hid.

BISHOP: Forgive us, Lord. We knew not what we did.

The DEVILS swagger menacingly, only to flee as JESUS makes his gesture of release. The BISHOP, unbound, kneels in prayer.

DEVILS lead forward the bound GOOSE MAGDALENE.

SATAN: Yah! But you cannot deny me this Whore.
    Tonight in Hell this Goose shall roast.
    No wicked Witch ever sinned more.

JESUS: She never blasphemed the Holy Ghost.
    She is the Keeper of my Secret Door.

SATAN: I grant you she let in more Men than most,
    And now it's my turn to give her what for.

JESUS: Ha! The horny man and his hollow boast!
    Now back off you old letch!
    I'll not cast my pearls to swine.
    For I am come to fetch
    And ferry home what's mine.

JESUS makes the ritual gesture at THE GOOSE / MAGDALENE. Her bonds are miraculously broken. She prostrates herself before him. JESUS gently helps her to her feet.

SATAN: Go on! Filch The Goose, but grant me this Crow
    To stake and skewer and sizzle on spit.

JESUS: Repent, John Crow. If not, you must know:
    Not lust - but pride – shall be your mortal deficit.

SATAN: For he did forsake you, a-courtin' to go
    With some kinky Goose Goddess who got off her kit.

JESUS: Not lust, but Love, did in Her Garden grow.
    His Goddess of Mercy was my Holy Spirit.
    And was he too not tried
    In his travails with The Goose.
    The trickster nearly died
    Yet survived to slip the noose.

*JESUS makes the ritual gesture. JOHN CROW's bonds are
broken. He bows respectfully to JESUS, who embraces him.*

SATAN: For all your trickster talk
    I give not a turd.
    Methinks this pair of cony-catchers
    Have ensnared thee.
    Methinks your Judgement
    Becometh somewhat blurred
    From too long a-stewin'
    In the fleshpots of their Liberty.
    Do you not see
    How they do twist your every Word
    To sanctify their own pernicious heresy?

JESUS: Yet when I called them, I saw how they heard
    And harkened and opened their hearts to me.

SATAN: So they gave you a room.
    Well I don't give a fart.
    Are you the God of Doom,
    Or God of the Bleeding Heart?

JESUS: Of the weak and the sick,
    Of the wounded and broken,
    I will use every trick
    To pry the shell open.

SATAN: Who would want such a pearl,
  Fouled and festered in Thames mud?

JESUS: I would want such a pearl.
  It is washed clean with my blood.

SATAN: I don't believe I'm hearing this!
  Jaysus Christus!
  When he's not Deus ex Machina,
  He's Deus Sado-Masochismus!

JESUS: And thou the Accuser,
  That self-same Child Abuser,
  Who seeks but to shackle these Spirits in Sin,
  Doomed to dwell in dread and doubt
  Of the God you locked without,
  To whom I now reveal the God within.

SATAN: Not so fast, my friend, a pox on the past!
  In present time, you shall be smit!

SATAN advances. JESUS "freezes" him with the sign of the cross.

JESUS: Michael, Margaret. Hold him fast
  And bind the fiend that he not flit...

MICHAEL and MARGARET, as Angels, advance on SATAN, binding him in chains. THE GHASTLY CHERUB, set free from his bonds, blows his trumpet. ANGELS appear, overwhelming and binding BEELZEBUB and the DEVILS.

JESUS: With his own chains, let him be cast
  Into his fire and brimstone Pit.

SATAN: Ow! Ow! Harrow! And damn and blast!
  I sink into mine own Hell Pit.

SATAN sinks into the pit. ANGELS cast BEELZEBUB and the other DEVILS into the pit (cage).

BEELZEBUB: Alas! Alack! Alack! Alas!
  I stand at end of all my wit.

DEVILS: We cannot stand. We needs must sit.
  Now we are really in the shit.

The DEVILS are wheeled off in the cage. The BISHOP censes.

JESUS: Now... All you who wait in dread
    To know if saved or damned you be.
    When all that to me you did or said
    Stands naked in eternity.

JESUS surveys the audience, addressing them directly as the saved.

When I was hungry, you me fed.
    To slake my thirst your heart was free.
    Homeless I was, and wearied,
    You opened up your heart to me.
    When on my cross I wept and bled
    Then on my pain you took pity.
    When I was sick and took to bed
    Kindly you came to comfort me.

MOLL CUTPURSE answers for the saved.

MOLL: When did we, Lord that all has wrought,
    Bring meat and drink you for to feed?
    Did we poor misers spare one thought
    When you on cross did weep and bleed?
    Tell us, when have we ever brought
    You comfort in your time of need?
    When you were sick, you say we sought.
    Lord, when did we this good deed?

JESUS: My blessed children, I shall say
    When your good deed was to me done.
    When man or woman, night or day,
    Asked for your help, your heart not stone,
    Did not pass by or turn away,
    You saw that, in me, they too are One.
    But you that cursed them, said them nay,
    Your curse did cut me to the bone.

He surveys the audience severely, addressing them as the damned.

When I had need of meat and drink,
    You offered me an empty plate.

When I was clasped and chained in Clink,
You frowned, and left me to my fate.
Where I was teetering on the brink,
Did bolt and bar your iron gate.
When I was drowning, you let me sink.
When I cried for help, you came too late.

JOHN TAYLOR answers for the damned.

TAYLOR: When had you, Lord who all things has,
Hunger or thirst, or helplessness?
Had we but known God a prisoner was
We would surely have sought to ease His distress.
How could God be sick or dying? Alas!
When was He hungry, thirsty, or homeless?
How could such things come to pass?
When did we to thee such wickedness?

JESUS: Dead souls! When any bid
You pity them, you did but blame.
You heard them not, your heart you hid.
Your guilt told you they should be shamed.
Your thought was but the earth to rid
Of them I am now come to claim.
To the poorest wretch, whate'er you did,
To me you did the self and same.

PETER: Lord, if you would but make it clear
How each soul may be named and known.

JESUS: He that has ears to hear, let him hear,
Then let him judge himself alone.

*JESUS leads JOHN CROW forward, presenting him to
the audience.*

JESUS: As for mad John Crow
A Lost Soul, we all know
Yet he lived to give my Church a good Goosing.
And in his own crooked way
He turned out to play
His part in these Acts of Binding and Loosing.

For all over the World
My Children at Liberty

Are working to bind,
Or else working to loose.
Though the lamps be many
They light up my One Mind.

In Southwark I find me
My Winchester Goose.

*He leads THE GOOSE/MAGDALENE forward, presenting
her to the audience.*

With my blood she was bought
As in flesh she was framed.

GOOSE: By the curlies and short
    Men had me in your Name.
    I did call you in thought.

JESUS: And, as promised, I came.
    Thus, as God has sought
    So has he reclaimed.

GOOSE: Then I did not for nought.

JESUS: You have opened my heart.

CROW: Thus my Goose played her part in God's Game.

*JESUS joins the hands of THE GOOSE/MAGDALENE and
JOHN CROW in mystic marriage.*

JESUS: In you, I do marry
    The Flesh and the Spirit,
    That the Child here and now
    The Kingdom inherit.

For how can God ever resolve the Mystery
Of where he ends and where Man begins?
Until here and now in the State of Liberty
He heal his own rift in Forgiveness of Sins.

Until He's no longer "something out there".
Until We Are One Within.
Until We stop waiting for the end of the world,
And let it begin…

Epilogue

*The CHOIR sings. JOHN CROW recites verses from **The Book of The Magdalene**.*

CHOIR: She is come... She is come...
　　　She is come... She is come...

CROW: She is come out of Egypt by Greenwich,
　　　Upriver, the Dogs to her right,
　　　Along the black beach
　　　Around Limehouse Reach,
　　　With the City of London in sight.

　　　In Cathedral Provost may ponder
　　　If he should unbar the Great Door,
　　　With a wink and a nod
　　　To the Glory of God
　　　In the guise of an unredeemed Whore.

　　　Let Bishop's crook offer him Counsel,
　　　Ways and Means for the Door to unjam.
　　　If needs must be seen
　　　That the Whore be washed clean
　　　Of her Sin by the Blood of the Lamb,

　　　Then let it be so, but then let it go
　　　The Guilt and the Shame and the Sin.
　　　Let go of the Law
　　　That made her a Whore
　　　And then, for God's sake, let her in.

　　　Let in, let in, let no colour of skin
　　　Nor creed debar Other from ceremony.
　　　Let the gong of Tibet
　　　Bong out an octet
　　　With the Bells of St Mary Overie.

*A Tibetan gong sounds. Everybody makes the drone sound "O".
Buddhists intone the mantra, "OM MANI PADME HUM".*

GOOSE: And Now It Is Time To Call
   Time!
   Last orders, please! Millennium?
   Closing, gents, come on, drink up!
   Hurry up, please the ferryman
   Is waiting down at Stew Lane steps
   Waiting to row you over, dear,
   Waiting to find you Over There
   And so to row you...

COMPANY: Over 'ere!

The GOOSE recites **The Pilgrim's Way**.

GOOSE: Let not the Letter of the Law
   Deny the Spirit, Liberty.
   Nor burn my Book of Pictures
   Which it take for rank idolatry.
   For I am the Mistress Southwark,
   Am the Daughter of Eternity,
   And in me the Broken Man
   Shall be made whole, as merrily
   We wenden on our Pilgrimage,
   Who knows what wonders yet to see
   Along the winding track of Time
   On our journey home from Canterbury...

COMPANY: To Southwark!

The bells of Southwark Cathedral peal.

Appendix A

Penitential Procession

Option to move the audience out of the theatre at the end of **The Creations and Fall.**

CROMWELL: Then... It must be...

SATAN: It is! It is! It is the Day of Doom.

Thunder and lightning. They mill about in confusion. Enter KING HENRY VIII, pursued by a BEAR, unleashing panic in the pit.

KING: Help! Ho! Hunks of the Bear Garden! The Beast is loose!

Exit KING, pursued by the BEAR. In the confusion, MICHAEL and MARGARET slip the PURITAN SOLDIERS' clutches and run out of the theatre.

CROMWELL: Stop the brats!

Two of the SOLDIERS give chase.

The theatre is closed!

CROMWELL and SOLDIERS drag off JOHN CROW and THE GOOSE, herding the other PLAYERS behind them. The DEVIL'S BAND accompanies SATAN's triumphal exit. A POLICE CONSTABLE takes the stage (as at the end of **Lazarus***), appealing for calm through a megaphone.*

CONSTABLE: Ladies and gentlemen,
We don't wish to spoil your fun
Or in these works to cast a spanner.
We would merely ask
That what must needs be done.
Be done in a dignified manner... &c.

CONSTABLES and STEWARDS supervise the evacuation of the theatre.

The Penitential Procession of the Whore and the Heretic

East along Bankside, headed by the DEVIL'S BAND playing a march, and the BEAR, now chained and forced to dance. THE GOOSE, her head shaved, is paraded in a cart. JOHN CROW, stripped and tied to the back of the cart, is whipped by a man in a monkey mask. Bringing up the rear, a man in a death mask with a sandwich-board proclaiming "The End Is Nigh". A fickle, armed MOB tags along, alternately mocking the Whore, the Heretic and the escort of PURITAN SOLDIERS. CHARITY pushes her way through the crowd.

CHARITY: Hey, John Crow! What 'appenin', bro'? I warn you not to go messin' wi' the Mysteries. Done mash up your brains, boy! You forget to take your tablet, or what? Hey, leave 'im alone! Boy don't need a whippin'. He need Care in the Community.

The PURITAN SOLDIERS hustle CHARITY away. The processions continues, encountering a band of MEDIEVAL PILGRIMS. They fall to their knees, making the sign of the cross. JOHN CROW, whipped behind the cart, staggers and falls. GEFFREY CHAUCER runs to help him.

GEFFREY: Woah! Woah! For Christ's sake! He's foaming at the mouth.

GEFFREY and THE GOOSE help JOHN CROW up onto the cart. The MOB cheers and applauds. The PURITAN SOLDIERS exchange nervous looks.

GOOSE: Thanks, darlin'. Hang about... Geffrey?

GEFFREY: Goose?

GOOSE: Master Geffrey!

They embrace like old friends, laughing. The procession moves tentatively forward, with JOHN CROW now on the cart with THE GOOSE. He sits up, eyeing GEFFREY who walks alongside. JOHN TAYLOR and MOLL CUTPURSE observe THE GOOSE's introductions.

Er... John, Geffrey. Geffrey, John.

TAYLOR: (*Aside to MOLL.*) Geffrey Chaucer, your
   Canterbury Tales man. His Pilgrims set off from the old
   Tabard Inn, down Borough High Street.

MOLL: I dunno! John Crow, Will Shagspur, now old Jeff.
   Had 'em all, ain't she?

TAYLOR: Moll! What did I tell you? It's Symbolical, right?

MOLL: O... right.

*THE GOOSE stands on the cart, casting her spell on the
PILGRIMS, SOLDIERS and MOB with verses from **The
Book of The Goose**.*

GOOSE: Yes I been 'ere before, dear,
   Oft'times in chastened circumstance.
   I lay with Master Geffrey
   At the Tabard, making dalliance
   Afore wending on his Pilgrimage
   To tell a Tale of Canterbury
   And I rode out beside him
   As the Childe of Mary Overie...
   Went riding for a Vision,
   A Vision of Humanity,
   Man God and Beast communing
   For one moment in Eternity...

*The DEVIL'S BAND strike up a lyrical canon. The procession
takes on the air of a joyous Pilgrimage. JOHN CROW staggers
to his feet, in trance, speaking in tongues.*

CROW: And Southwark shall arise
   Naked in Her Liberty,
   On the South Bank of the Thames,
   Arrayed in all Her finery,
   With all Her Children
   Endowed with grace and dignity,
   The deformed and the deviant
   Embraced into Her Unity...

The music peters out as CROMWELL pushes through the crowd to halt the procession, appalled by what he sees. JOHN CROW continues prophesying, lost in his own world.

With One Voice shall speak Her Name,
And her name is Liberty!

CROMWELL jumps on the cart, punching JOHN CROW in the face, knocking him out.

CROMWELL: And Lo! The Lord hath struck him down for his Goose's Heresy. And get that bloody bear out of here! Did I not ban the baiting of bears on Bankside?

The BEAR is led away. The MOB murmurs its disapproval.

Aye, call us killjoys, but some joys must be killed, or
Man's no more than that poor, slavering beast. Shall
honest wives wait at home, while their husbands consort
with whores? You want to see your grandmothers raped
by drug-crazed children? A world where God is dead
and nothing is forbidden?
(*To SOLDIERS.*) Go on, then, loose the Witch,
Let the whole World go to Hell!
This Harlot has the lot of you under her spell.

GEFFREY: Goose, what on Earth have you been doing?

GOOSE: The Puritans are up in arms.
I need poets to defend me.
It's time to tell The Goose's Tale...
Help! Master Geffrey!

The procession, stripped of the BEAR and other profanities, moves on. GEFFREY follows. A trumpet sounds. Distant voices.

VOICES: He is come! He is come!

CROMWELL: He is come. And we
To meet our Maker must go.
Let us pray we escape the fate that awaits
This Southwark Goose and her Crow.

*The PLAYERS and audience arrive at a new site for **The Second Coming** to discover JESUS, a rough sleeper. All Sing.*

CHOIR: He is come... He is come...
   He is come... He is come...

*Scene continues: see **Mary Magdalene***

Appendix B

The Houses of Healing

Option to take the audience out of the theatre during **The Houses of Healing**.

The **Healing The Dragon** scene begins in the theatre. The MUMMERS and SISTERS OF REDCROSS lead the audience out, in procession.

For a specified time, punters choose between alternative, site-specific *Houses of Healing*, before converging on the main *House* (**Thomas' and Guy's**). The "Houses" may be fairground booths clustered around a main performance site, or separate locations around Bankside, marked on a map included in the programme. The performers may devise their own Houses of Healing to complement the following suggested scenarios.

The Mass House

A representation of the secret Catholic Mass House in Kent Lane (now Tabard Street). The PRIEST's robes and ritual objects are carefully removed from hiding places under the floorboards. The PRIEST is robed and commences to perform the Mass. The old Irish NAVIGATOR interprets the scene for the audience.

The House of Reminiscence

A gutted warehouse. Smoke lingering in the air. FIREMEN and CIVIL DEFENCE WORKERS sift through rubble. TED and LIL, Southwark pensioners, recall their wedding during the blitz, ad lib. Their wedding night in the Borough tube air-raid shelter. The reception at Ted's Mum's. The bomb that blew soot down the chimney all over the cake. "We had a black wedding cake! Lil dusted it down. Shame to waste it!" They roar with laughter. TED has a coughing fit. Through the mist, CIVIL DEFENCE WORKERS stretcher out a wounded child.

The Stew

At the door, sexy DEVILS warn the punters that the show is for "Consenting Adults Only". Inside, a room draped in scarlet, with a heart-shaped bed, an altar with a skull, candles, smouldering incense. A CROW shaman and a tantric GOOSE perform **The Book of The Game** and **The Book Of The Honest John**, celebrating the sacred art of sexual healing.

The House of Revelation

A vagabond CROW and bag-lady GOOSE perform **The Bankside Book of Revelation**.

The House of The Nightingales

A bare cell, enclosed garden or courtyard, representing the Convent of St Mary Overie. A CHOIR of NIGHTINGALES sing **The Ballad of Mary Overie** and plainchant from *A Feather On The Breath of God* by Hildegard of Bingen. The nurse MARY SEACOLE teaches ST GEORGE how to dress and bandage a wound.

The House of the Senses

An installation created and operated by CHILDREN, who are directed by MICHAEL and MARGARET. Individual punters are blindfolded and led through a sensory environment. The children form "touch tunnels", touching the participants, tickling their faces with feathers, letting them smell flowers and other fragrances, placing unfamiliar objects in their hands. Others create soundscapes. At the end of the tunnel, the blindfolds are removed. The punters stand in a room bathed in sequences of "healing" colours, viewing the installation.

The House of the Hungry Ghosts

MARY MAGDALENE silently tends a shrine, lighting candles and burning incense. A nearby soup-kitchen dispenses free food to the needy.

Guy's Chapel

An ecumenical service, conducted by a female minister, conferring blessings on St Thomas' and Guy's Hospitals. Poems and songs are recited in honour of St Mary Magdalene. The address deconstructs the traditional image of the penitent whore, stressing her role as the Apostle of the apostles, the woman "who anointed our Lord for death". Mention is made of her parish and church in Bermondsey. Candles are lit and the names and photographs of those in need of healing are placed before the mural of the Magdalene with her pot of ointment.

The Temple of Isis

Green light bathes a cavernous room. On a simple stone altar: a Roman jug; a candle; incense. Chalked on the walls: glyphs and symbols; the legend LONDINI AD FANUM ISIDIS; the names "Goose", "Mary", "Isis", "Magdala in Overie"; and, on facing walls, two contrary inscriptions: "Blessed are the wombs that are fruitful" and "Blessed are the wombs that are barren." On a hospital-bed: the lifeless body of OSIRIS, hooked up to a drip. ISIS and THOTH, as Egyptian deities, perform the rites of death and rebirth. The scene is performed cyclically. The AUDIENCE are admitted in small groups, as silent witnesses and initiates to the Mystery.

see **THE MYSTERY PLAYS: The Houses of Healing: The Temple of Isis**

The Hallowing of Crossbones

The caverns under the arches of London Bridge station. PARTICIPANTS are greeted by GOOSE HOSTESSES and given a ribbon bearing the name of someone buried at Crossbones (from London Metropolitan Archives). CROW PRIESTESSES admit them to the inner chamber to leave mementoes on the Altar to the Ancestors. THE GOOSE and JOHN CROW perform *The Vision Books of The Goose, Crow, New South Bank, Honest John* and *Magdalene* in a ritual drama retelling the secret history of Crossbones and its reawakening.

The performance culminates in a candlelit procession to the gates of Crossbones Graveyard. The names of the dead are read aloud, as all tie their ribbons to the shrine at the gates. All recite: "Here lay your hearts, your flowers, your Book of Hours..." then sing **John Crow's Riddle** and **The Ballad of Mary Overie**. The ritual is closed with the pouring of a libation of gin and, call-and-response, the blessing: "Goose may you never be hungry. Goose may you never be thirsty. Goose may your spirit fly free."

At the end of the time allocated for the individual Houses of Healing, a bell or gong sounds, summoning the performers and audience to the main performance site. **The Houses of Healing** climaxes with **Thomas' and Guy's**, **Judas Iscariot** and **Lazarus**, performed in the grounds of Guy's Hospital.

Appendix C

The Egyptian Mystery Play

*Optional performance as part of **The Penitential Procession** or **The Houses of Healing**.*

A quasi-medieval Mystery Play performed on a cart by the river. Onstage, the Court of Pharoah. MOSES petitions PHAROAH.

MOSES: King Pharoah, now you must relent!

PHAROAH: Why, what tidings canst thou tell?

MOSES: From God in Heaven am I sent
To fetch his folk of Israel
To wilderness he would they went.

PHAROAH: Yah! Wend thou to the dwell of hell;
I'll give your folk cause to repent,
For in my danger shall they dwell.
And, trickster, for thy sake
They shall be put to pine.

MOSES: Our God shall vengeance take
On thee and all of thine.

Exit MOSES. PHAROAH is left alone onstage, brooding. THE GOOSE provides an offstage commentary, prompting JOHN CROW and the punters to recall the story.

GOOSE: Moses, remember? Basket in the bullrushes? Who finds him? Pharoah's daughter. So Moses is raised by the Priests of the One God, Aten. Now the Egyptians, they got the technology to carve in stone. Did someone mention Tablets of the Law? They prime the boy's mind, as a weapon in their war on Hathor, Great Mother. On the male-female gods of the One made Many. Moses learned his lesson well – then he set out on his own way.

Enter EGYPTIANS, reporting the bad news to PHAROAH.

1ST EGYPTIAN: Alas! Alas! This land is 'lorn
  On life we may no longer lend.

2ND EGYPTIAN: So great mischief is made since morn
  There may no medicine amend.

3RD EGYPTIAN: Sir King, we ban that we were born
  Our bliss with baleful bile is blend.

PHAROAH: Why cry you so, lads? List you scorn?

1ST EGYPTIAN: Sir King, such care was never kenned.
  The Nile, that waters man and beast,
  Makes fertile Egypt in its flood,
  Fresh-water fouled and scummed with yeast
  Does froth and foam, is gorged with blood.
  Full ugly and full ill is it
  That was full fair and fresh before.

PHAROAH: This is great wonder for to wit
  Of all the works that ever wore.

2ND EGYPTIAN: Nay, Pharoah, there be others yet
  That hex and vex and fret us sore
  A plague of toads and frogs, once bit
  Their venom… kills us… less… or more…

*Second EGYPTIAN loses his thread, distracted by THE
GOOSE's offstage commentary.*

GOOSE: So Moses leads the Children of Israel out of Egypt.
  Remember? The parting of the Red Sea.

JOHN CROW joins in the offstage conversation.

CROW: These Bankside Mummers, their budget will
  not stretch
  To some Cecil B. de Mille type parting of the Thames.

GOOSE: No shortage of Watermen to ferry 'em over.
  Except the Tribe what fetched up here was Egyptians.

PHAROAH and the EGYPTIANS have all dropped out of character, glowering at THE GOOSE.

PHAROAH: Madam, we are poor painted players
Mumming this masque of Mystery.
Perhaps you would care to step up and take over
Since you seem so acquainted with our Secret History.

GOOSE: Very civil of you. Don't mind if I do.

THE GOOSE climbs up on the cart.

GOOSE: So... Moses says he'll lead them to a Land of milk and honey? Only when they get to Sinai, it's a desert. What to do? We fall back on what we know. Hathor. The Cow Goddess? We make the Golden Calf. We do the ceremony. So Moses gets the hump, stomps off up to the mountain, gets the burning bush – WHOOOSH! Ten Commandments set in Tablets of Stone: "I am the Lord thy God. Thou Shalt Have No Other God But Me."

PHAROAH: Do you then deny the God of Israel?
The God of Moses and the Moral Law?

GOOSE: Each Tribe must be true to its own Divinity,
And do what it can to heal the old rift.
We know about Israel, the Egyptian captivity,
But what became of the Children of Egypt?

*THE GOOSE sings from **The Book of the Egyptian**.*

As in Israel come out of Egypt,
So in Egypt come out of Rome,
The ferryman's daughter... &c.

THE BALLAD OF MARIE OVERIE

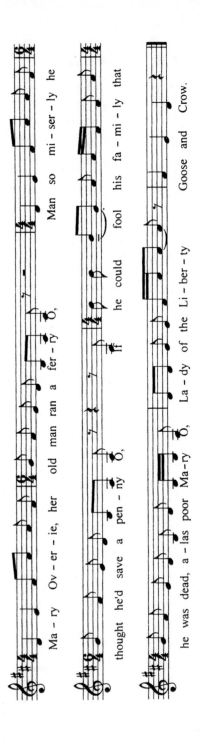

Ma – ry Ov – er – ie, her old man ran a fer – ry O, Man so mi – ser – ly he

thought he'd save a pen – ny O, If he could fool his fa – mi – ly that

he was dead, a – las poor Ma – ry O, La – dy of the Li – ber – ty Goose and Crow.

John Constable
Arrangement by Richard Kilgour.

THE GOOSE OF SOUTHWARK

Richard Kilgour.

JOHN CROW'S RIDDLE

John Crow with a rid-dle in a mad cap rhyme, Here to re-veal my My-ste-ry. In Lon-don Town at the end of time,

Johnny go down on his-tor-y   For to night in hell they are toll-ing the bell for the Whore that lay at the Tab ard. And

well we know that the car-ri-on crow doth feast in our Cross bones grave yard,   With a   Hey Ho,   jol-ly Jack Crow and his

mer-ry, mer-ry band of out-laws O,   Ne-ver stum-ble when he trips, Mad clown of the A-poc-a-lypse.

John Constable
Arrangement by Richard Kilgour.

THE BOOK OF THE CROW

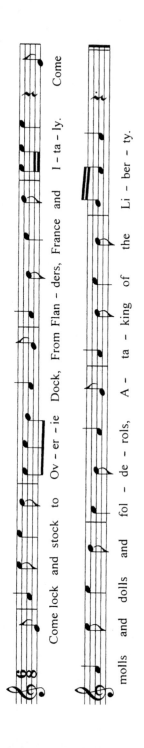

Come lock and stock to Ov – er – ie Dock, From Flan – ders, France and I – ta – ly. Come

molls and dolls and fol – de – rols, A – ta – king of the Li – ber – ty.

John Constable
Arrangement by Richard Kilgour.

GLOSSOLALIA

Author's Note

At the heart of the Mysteries is a matrix of living energies and intelligences, interacting across Space and Time to heal the primordial rift between the Flesh and the Spirit. To reunite the Tantric Tribe. To reassemble the Body of Christ in the Temple of Isis. And to transform Samsara, the illusory world of names and forms that commonly passes for reality.

As in a conventional glossary, highlighted words (marked in bold) cross-refer to other entries. If this rule were strictly enforced much of the text would be highlighted, since all of the entries ultimately interconnect. It is for this reason that only selected link-words have been highlighted, creating a lattice of pathways, narrative threads through the Secret History.

Reader, be aware. This is the trick of a Whore and a Whore's Prophet, the chase of a wild Goose.

ABBEY, The: Bermondsey Abbey, dedicated to **St Saviour**, founded in 1089. In 1117 the monks found a Saxon cross in the Thames mud, which they believed had fallen from heaven. The relic came to be venerated as the Holy Rood of St Saviour. King Henry II spent Christmas at the Abbey in 1154, seven years before authorising the **Ordinances** relating to the **stews**. Following the 1539 dissolution of the monasteries, the Abbey was demolished.

ABRAHAM: (or Abram, Ibrahim.) Hebrew, Christian and Muslim patriarch. He was tested by God, who demanded that he sacrifice his son, Isaac. Orthodox Christians regard him as an exemplar of man's submission to God's will. The Chester **Mystery Plays** interpret the story as prefiguring God's sacrifice of his own son, Jesus. In the Southwark Cycle, John Crow cites it as evidence that **Yahweh** is the false God of human sacrifice.

ACTORS: The names of more than half the actors appearing in **Shakespeare**'s *First Folio* are listed in the parish records of **St Saviour's**. In 1547, Gardiner, Bishop of **Winchester**, complained of the Bankside actors' intention to compete with his "solemn mass" for the late King Henry VIII by performing "a solemn play, to try who shall have the most resort, they in game or I in earnest". The Burbage family "relocated" **The Globe** to **Bankside**, where Richard Burbage performed the roles of Hamlet, Othello and King Lear. In *The Southwark Mysteries*, actors and **whores** are invoked as the guardians of Bankside's ancient hermetic traditions. They were traditionally regarded as natural bedfellows, engaged in equally disreputable professions, both of which flourished outside the **City**'s strict licensing laws. The Lord Mayor of London regularly petitioned Queen Elizabeth I's Privy Council to ban all plays, protesting that:

> Our apprentices and servants are by this means corrupted and induced hereby to defraud their masters, to maintain their vain and prodigal expenses occasioned by such evil and riotous company, where into they fall by these meetings.

In *Holland's Leaguer* (1632), the procuress Dona Hollandia:
> ... was most taken with the report of three famous amphitheatres, which stood so near situated that her eye might take view of them from the lowest turret. One was the Continent of the World (The Globe) because half the year a world of beauties and brave spirits resorted to it...

Philip Henslowe and his stepson-in-law Edward "Ned" Alleyn supplemented their incomes as **theatre** and **bear-baiting** impresarios with a bit of brothel-keeping on the side. In 1593 Ned Alleyn's wife, Joan Woodward, was imprisoned in the **Clink** for keeping a bawdy house and "by my Lord Mayor's officer made to ride in a cart".

ADAM: The first man of Judaeo-Christian theology. The book of Genesis conflates two distinct accounts of his origins. In the first, the Primal Ancestor is endowed with male and female attributes: "God created man in his own image... male and female created he them" (Genesis 1: 27). In the second: "The Lord God formed man out of the dust of the ground, and breathed into his nostrils the breath of life; and man became a living soul..." (Genesis 2: 7). Having set man in the garden of Eden, forbidding him to eat of the tree of knowledge, God "caused a deep sleep to fall upon Adam, and he slept: and he took one of his ribs, and closed up the flesh... (and) ...made he a woman..." (Genesis 2: 21–22). Beguiled by the serpent, the woman persuaded Adam to break God's commandment, precipitating their expulsion from Eden. The **Gnostic** *Apocalypse of Adam* tells a very different story: "God" himself is already "fallen". Adam tells his son Seth how:
> Eve your mother... taught me a word of knowledge of the eternal god. And we resembled the great eternal angels, for we were higher than the god who had created us and the powers with him, whom we did not know.

and of their own fall, how:
> The eternal knowledge of the god of truth withdrew from me and your Mother Eve. Since that time we learnt about dead things, like men. Then we recognised the god who had created us. For we were not strangers to his powers. And we served him in fear and slavery.

This is a common thread of Gnostic creation myths: Adam and Eve fall into "the Sleep of Death" and, forgetting their own divinity, begin worshipping the false creator god. According to the *Gospel of Philip*: "Men make gods and worship their creation. It would be fitting for the gods to worship men!" This concept – of a divine man who originally contained heaven and earth within himself, but, projecting himself onto the created universe, became the slave of a god of his own creation – found vivid expression in the prophetic poems of **William Blake**.

AKASHIC RECORDS: One of the lower levels of the **astral plane**, a "psychic library" where human thought-forms are recorded in eternity. It could be said to correspond with Dr Karl Popper's world of the "objective contents of thoughts." In **I Was An Alien Sex God**, John Crow's mentor, Sir Henry Halfhide, extrapolates:

> The ancients, dear boy, the Egyptians... They believed that everything we think is recorded on the Astral Plane... These 'Akashic Records' can be read, and the secrets of men's souls laid bare. Ah yes, on the Astral, our thoughts take on a life of their own. My dear, you should see some of mine!

ALE-HOUSES: As a medieval staging-post for travellers and pilgrims, the old Borough was well-endowed with **taverns** and coaching-inns (see **Tabard Inn, The**). **Chaucer**'s Miller famously sampled the local brew:

> And if my words get muddled in my tale
> Just put it down to too much Southwark ale.

St. Margaret's Hill (later Borough High Street) was described by Thomas Dekker as "one continued ale-house". A survey in 1631 listed 288 ale-houses, of which some 43 were suppressed on the grounds of plague or rowdiness.

ALI: "From **Costcutters**". Apocryphal shop-worker, invoked by **Jesus** in the Southwark Mystery Plays as an Islamic "Samaritan".

ANCHOR, The: The oldest surviving Bankside tavern, erected on the site of 'The Castle on the Hoope', a medieval **stew**, said by H. E. Popham to have been **Shakespeare**'s local: "He should have come here. He must have come here. Let us say, finally and definitely, that he did." In the eighteenth century, a local brewer and MP named Henry Thrale and his wife Hester hosted a literary salon here, where Dr Johnson regularly held forth to his biographer Boswell, the actor Garrick, the playwright Oliver Goldsmith and the philosopher Edmund Burke. Johnson, author of the first *Dictionary of the English Language*, took rooms at 'The Anchor', where he wrote his *Lives of the English Poets*. His relationship with the Thrales, whom he even escorted on holiday, excited much scandalised gossip.

APOCALYPSE: The revelation or "unveiling" of the "hidden things". The Jewish apocalyptic books date from c. 200 BCE–100 CE. Their influence can be seen in the **Revelation** of St John, wherein a vengeful God unleashes plagues, poisons and other abominations on sinful humanity. The **Gnostic** *Apocalypse of Peter* presents a more compassionate vision of the end of time, but was denied a place in canonical scripture. *The Southwark Mysteries* prophesy a world, not consumed by fire, but healed by water; the flesh transfigured by the spirit. (See **Millennium**.)

APPLE: In Jewish and Christian mythology, the forbidden fruit "of the tree of the knowledge of good and evil" (Genesis 2: 17) with which **Eve** was beguiled by the serpent (Genesis 3: 1–6). Christianity's ambivalence towards the act that ultimately unleashed the mystery of God's incarnation as "the Son of Man" can be seen in the anonymous fifteenth-century poem *O Felix Culpa*:

> Ne had the apple taken been,
> The apple taken been,
> Ne hadde never our Lady
> A been heaven's queen.
> Blessed be the time
> That apple taken was!

ARAB STRAP: Leather thong tied around the penis and testicles, used by prostitutes to reinforce their clients' erections during penetrative sex. The strap prevents the blood draining from the erectile tissue. It can also be looped around the balls in a figure-of-eight, separating and supporting them. As the name suggests, it was popularly believed to have been invented by the Arabs, and to have originally been made of camel hide.

ARACHNE: In Greek mythology, the Lydian maiden who challenged Athena in the art of weaving. The jealous goddess ripped her work to shreds, whereupon Arachne, in terror, committed suicide. Taking pity on her plight, Athena turned her into a spider. The rope from which she hung was transformed into a cobweb. Arachne became a folk goddess of spinsters, and, by association, **witches**. Some have suggested that "A", the scarlet letter of Nathaniel Hawthorne's novel, signifies not "Adulteress" but "Arachne".

ASTRAL PLANE: In esoteric tradition, the material world is but one of many. The astral plane is the realm of thought-forms, accessible only in the astral body. It is said that **The Goose** and **John Crow** are operating on the astral plane to effect certain alterations in the **Akashic Records**.

AYAHUASCA: (or Yage.) Psychoactive brew, concocted from an Amazonian vine and medicinal leaves, used by **shamans** to connect with the spirit world, specifically in healing ceremonies. **John Crow** was rumoured to have attended Ayahuasca ceremonies during 1998 and 1999.

BAILLY, Harry: The host of **The Tabard Inn**, in **Chaucer**'s *The Canterbury Tales*, was based on Henricus Bailly (or Baillif), a Southwark innkeeper and MP for the Borough. Fourteenth-century surnames often referred to the holder's occupation. We should not assume that Harry was related to his contemporaries Richard and Margery Bailif, two of the earliest recorded Southwark **stewholders**. In the Southwark Mystery Plays, Harry Bailly hosts the Last Supper.

BANKSIDE: Riverside thoroughfare on the south bank of the Thames, stretching roughly from what is now Blackfriars Bridge to London Bridge. From the twelfth to the seventeenth centuries it formed the northern boundary of Paris Garden and the **Liberty of the Clink**. In **Shakespeare**'s day, it was a waterfront strip of **taverns**, **stews**, bear-pits and **theatres**, backed by tenter-grounds, fishponds, fields, orchards and market-gardens. Its squalid **rents** and yards teemed with actors, whores, cut-purses and cut-throats – all preying on the men who came over the river in search of forbidden pleasures. The suppression of its bear-pits, brothels and theatres under **Cromwell** and the Puritans coincided with the sale of the Bishop of **Winchester**'s lands to property developers (1647–9). With the restoration of Charles II in 1660, London's theatreland moved back across the river to Drury Lane. By the eighteenth century the Bankside was an industrial waterfront of wharves, warehouses and overcrowded tenement slums. During the Second World War, German bombs flattened the Southwark and Bermondsey docks. With the closure of the wharves in the early 1970s, the area seemed to be in terminal decline. The 1980s saw the development of tracts of derelict land, attracting national and international companies to The **Borough**. Bankside's "regeneration" accelerated during the 1990s with the reconstruction of Shakespeare's Globe, the refurbishment of the **New Bankside Power** Station as the Tate Gallery of Modern Art, a 'Millennium Footbridge' linking Bankside with St Paul's, **Southwark Cathedral**'s new visitor's centre, and the **Jubilee** Line Extension. Local residents expressed concern that Bankside was being turned into one vast **Heritage Theme Park**.

BANKSIDE BOOK OF REVELATION, The: John Crow's satirical reply to the book of **Revelation**, explicitly aimed at those who interpret it literally.

BANKSIDE ORATORY: Possibly **The Anchor**, where Dr Johnson held forth at Mrs Thrale's literary salon. Some claim it was from here that, on 6 September 1666, the diarist Samuel Pepys watched the Great Fire of London from the safety of "a little ale-house on the Bankside".

BCE: Before the Christian Era. Abbreviation used in this glossary as an alternative to the archaic term BC (Before Christ).

BEAR: "Quadruped of the order *Carnivora*, with long shaggy hair and hooked claws; any rude, rough, or ill-bred fellow... fig: a broker speculating on a fall in stock-prices, as opposed to Bull." (*Chambers Twentieth Century Dictionary*, 1901)

BEAR-BAITING: Popular "sport" in Tudor and Stuart England. Spectators were seated in galleries around a pit, where the bear was tied to a stake and set upon by dogs. **Bankside** offered many variants of the sport, including "whipping of the blind bear". A blind bear named Harry Hunks features in a poem by Henry Peacham, written in 1611: "Hunks of the Beare-garden to be feared..." When King Henry VIII attended a bear-baiting in 1539, the bear broke loose and climbed into a boat, which overturned. The architecture of **The Globe** and other Bankside **theatres** was influenced by the bear-pits which partly subsidised them. The **actor-** manager Ned Alleyn was also a bear-baiting impresario. In 1604 he was appointed Master of the Royal Bears, Bulls and Mastiffs. His father-in-law Philip Henslowe built The Hope as a dual-purpose theatre and bear-pit close to The Rose and The Globe theatres. We may imagine the panic unleashed by Shakespeare's most famous stage direction: "exit pursued by a bear." During 1996, The Globe Education Centre was housed within the footprint of The Hope in Bear Gardens; a huge stuffed bear stood in the lobby.

BEDLAM: (or Bethlem Hospital.) London's infamous "mental asylum", immortalised in the ballads of **Tom o' Bedlam**:

> On the lordly lofts of Bedlam
> With stubble soft and dainty,
> Brave bracelets strong, sweet whips ding-dong,
> And wholesome hunger plenty.

In his *Amusements Serious and Comical, Calculated for the Meridian of London* (1700), Tom Brown presents it as a freak-show for the amusement and edification of polite Georgian society:

> Some were praying, others cursing and swearing. Some were dancing, others groaning. Some singing, others crying, and all in perfect confusion. A sad representation of the greater chimerical world.

Twentieth-century social reformers campaigned for the closure of such institutions, but the "Care in the Community" initiative of the 1990s only resulted in confused and frightened inmates being discharged and left to fend for themselves. The hospital occupied four different sites, including **St George's Fields** (1815–1930). Parts of the original building were incorporated into the **Imperial War Museum**.

BEELZEBUB: "The Lord of the Flies". In Mark 3: 22–23, where Christ is accused of serving him, Beelzebub is **Satan** by another name:

> And the scribes which came down from Jerusalem said, He hath Beelzebub, and by the prince of the devils casteth he out devils. And (Jesus) called them unto him, and said unto them in parables, How can Satan cast out Satan?

The **Mystery Plays** depict him as a distinct, subordinate devil. In the Southwark Cycle, he is Satan's cack-handed sidekick.

BERMONDSEY: Parish and former metropolitan borough to the east of Southwark, extending from London Bridge to Rotherhithe. The name, derived from "the Isle of Beormond", dates back to when the south bank was marshland.

BINDING AND LOOSING: The spiritual authority invested in St Peter and the apostles by Christ (Matthew 16: 19 and 18: 18). In *The Southwark Mysteries*, "binding and loosing" is identified with the contrary states of "holding" and "releasing", and, specifically, with the mummification rites performed by **Isis** to resurrect the dismembered **Osiris**.

BISHOP: The British comic tradition of vicars and tarts, actresses and bishops may well derive from when the Bishops of **Winchester** licensed prostitutes within the medieval **Liberty of the Clink**.

BLACKFRIARS: Area on the north bank of the Thames, at the mouth of the Fleet, one of London's **lost rivers**. It takes its name from the black robes of the Dominican friars who founded a priory there – not to be confused with the Black Augustinian canons who inherited the Priory of **St Mary Overie**. (See **Southwark Cathedral**.) Blackfriars Road runs south from the Bridge, parallel to the boundary between Southwark and **Lambeth**.

BLACKFRIARS DITCH: Underground stream (see **lost rivers**) supposed to flow into the Thames from the south, near Blackfriars Bridge. Or perhaps an allusion to the "black ditch", an Elizabethan sewer that ran through **St Olave's**.

BLAKE, William: (1757–1827.) Visionary poet and painter. He had his first vision – of "a tree filled with angels" – at Peckham Rye. His belief that "all Deities reside in the Human Breast" displays striking affinities with **Gnosticism**. In *The Book of Urizen*, Blake's vicious parody of Genesis, a fallen demiurge imprisons humanity in the created universe of matter:

> Six days they shrunk up from existence
> And on the seventh day they rested,
> And they blessed the seventh day, in sick hope,
> And forgot their eternal life.

His **Jesus** is "Imagination", ceaselessly working to transform the natural world, to reveal "the Human Form Divine":

> Thou art a man, God is no more,
> Thy own humanity learn to adore
> For that is my Spirit of Life.

Blake lived seven years in **Lambeth**, where tales were told of his eccentric behaviour: he and his wife were once caught naked in their garden playing "Adam and Eve". On his way into the City he would have passed the soot-smeared Albion Mills on **Blackfriars** Road, believed by many to have been the "dark satanic mills" of *Jerusalem*. The poem, set to music by Parry, ironically became the anthem of the blinkered nationalism Blake so despised. His *Proverbs of Hell* celebrate the dynamic interplay of "contraries" in terms that would have delighted The Goose: "Prisons are built with stones of law, Brothels with bricks of Religion." A prolific painter and engraver, he illustrated Dante, Milton, the Bible and his own idiosyncratic vision world. One of his paintings, in the Tate Millbank, is entitled *Christ the Mediator, Christ pleading before the Father for St Mary Magdalene*. **The Goose's Prophecy** invokes him as a kindred spirit, in language that echoes his great prophetic poem, *Jerusalem*: "And Jerusalem is called Liberty among the Children of Albion."

BODY PARTS, Missing: The eighteenth century saw the establishment of teaching hospitals such as **St Thomas'** and **Guy's**. The study of anatomy was hampered by a shortage of corpses for dissection. Gangs of body snatchers, or "resurrectionists", would dig up recently buried bodies to sell to surgeons. The trade became so lucrative that the surgeons formed an Anatomy Club in an attempt to regulate spiralling prices. *The Southwark Mysteries* recalls the infamous **Borough Boys** and the 1998 trial of the body-snatching artist, Anthony Noel-Kelly, in **Southwark Crown Court**. The metaphor is used to explore Christianity's troubled relationship with the flesh. The medieval worship of relics is contrasted with the Rites of **Mary Overie**, sanctifying the sexual body of the living **Christ**.

BOROUGH, The: Medieval settlement to the south of **London Bridge**. It was never a "borough" in the strict legal sense, the **City** having persistently denied it the right to establish a Mayor, a Charter or a Town Council. The old Borough occupied a relatively confined area, bounded by marshes to the east (**Bermondsey**), west (**Lambeth**), and south (**St George's Fields**). As the marshes were drained, the conurbation sprawled southwards. By the nineteenthth century it had become dangerously overpopulated. The area was frequently razed by fire, and, during the Second World War, by German bombs. The name survives in an underground station, and is still used, mainly by locals, for the area around the church of **St George the Martyr**.

BOROUGH BOYS, The: Gang of Southwark body snatchers, led by Ben Crouch, a former prize-fighter. They provided specimens for Sir Astley Cooper, the great surgeon of **Guy's**, who spent a small fortune keeping them out of prison and maintaining the families of those serving sentences. Cooper eventually joined forces with Jeremy Bentham, author of *Auto-Icon, or the use of the dead to the living*, to press for reform of the law. Their campaign, fuelled by public outrage at the Burke and Hare scandal in Edinburgh, resulted in the Anatomy Act, which permitted the use of unclaimed corpses from workhouses. Ben Crouch and the Borough Boys promptly went on strike, to no avail. Legislation rapidly undermined the black-market in "stiffs". In 1833, Astley Cooper delivered Bentham's funeral oration. The deceased's instructions, that his body be preserved in a glass case, were followed to the letter. The resulting effigy can be seen in the foyer of University College, London. The head briefly went missing in a rag-day stunt, and was later discovered in Scotland. One version of the story has it turning up in the vice-chancellor's bed.

BREWING: In *The Canterbury Tales*, **Chaucer** alludes to the strength of the local brews dispensed in The Borough's **inns**, **taverns** and **ale-houses**:

> The nappy strong ale of Southwark
> Keeps many a gossip from the Kirk.

The old brewing dynasties included Leakes, Weblings, Monger, Child and the family of Henry Thrale, landlord of **The Anchor** and MP for Southwark. In 1955 one of the oldest breweries, Barclay and Perkins of Park Street, was taken over by Courage's, who had opened their Bermondsey brewery in 1787. The closure of Courage's in the 1980s marked the end of a centuries-old tradition. The imposing Hop Exchange on Southwark Street, erected in 1866, testifies to the former wealth and influence of the brewing industry.

BRID: (or Bride, Brigid.) Irish folk-saint (d. c.525), whose cult flourished throughout the Celtic diaspora. According to Gerald of Wales, a fire was kept burning at her shrine for centuries, surrounded by a circle of bushes, which no man was permitted to enter. Some commentators have identified her with the **goddess** Brig, whose fire-rites took place on 1 February, Brid's feast day. Her reported miracles read like pagan variations on Christ's own. Jesus multiplies the loaves. Brid does the same to the butter. At the marriage in Canaan, Jesus turns water into wine. When a party of thirsty priests shows up at her priory, Brid turns her dirty bath water into beer. Her most famous London church is St Bride's, Fleet Street. Its "wedding-cake" spire can be clearly seen from the mudflats on the south bank.

BRIDGES: The first lines of *The Book of The Crow* echo the grisly opening to **Dickens'** *Our Mutual Friend*, in which Gaffer Hexham and his daughter Lizzie search for the bodies of suicides "between Southwark Bridge which is of iron and London Bridge which is of stone." "Towers, London, Southwark, Blackfriars, Hungerford, Waterloo, Westminster, Lambeth" are the bridges spanning the Thames, as mapped from a hawk's eye view, flying upriver. The Millennium footbridge, linking **Bankside** with St Paul's, opened in 2000.

BRITANNIA HOUSE: Twentieth-century Inland Revenue office on Trinity Street, perhaps invoked as a symbol of the foundering nation state. The night security guard would have been a familiar face on **John Crow**'s nocturnal rambles between **Trinity Church Square** and the **Crossbones** graveyard.

BROKEN WING JOHN CROW: Sidekick of Anancy the Spider, the trickster hero of African and Caribbean folk tales, featured in **Constable**'s play *Black Mas.* In many cultures, the **shaman** is marked by physical and spiritual deformity, often assuming the name and form of a despised creature.

BUDDHA: The "enlightened" or "awakened one". Siddhartha Gautama was born c. 600 BCE into a Nepalese royal family. He married his cousin, Princess Yasodhara, who bore him a child, and lived a life of luxury until the age of 29, when he became deeply troubled by the human afflictions of old age, disease and death. Renouncing earthly possessions, he dedicated his life to freeing all beings from suffering. Having meditated for six years, he attained enlightenment under a bodhi tree in Bodhgaya, India. After his death, Buddhism spread throughout the East. The Theravada School, which flourished in Sri Lanka and South East Asia, was based on strict codes of conduct and the practice of Vipassana (mindfulness). The Mahayana School emphasised the Buddha nature innate in all sentient beings, and the infinite mercy of the Bodhisattva. (See **Kwan Yin**.) It evolved in Nepal, Tibet, China and Japan into diverse, esoteric disciplines, including **Tantra** and **Zen**. The dissemination of Buddhist ideas was accelerated by the 1959 Chinese invasion of Tibet, which forced many Lamas into exile. In 1997, London's oldest courthouse, close to the **Elephant and Castle**, was converted into the Jamyang Buddhist Centre, with a statue of the Buddha seated on the former judge's dais. Two years later, the Dalai Lama opened the Tibetan Peace Garden adjacent to the **Imperial War Museum**.

BURFORD, Ephraim J: Twentieth-century social historian, specialising in London low-life. His book *Bawds and Lodgings* (1976, republished as *The Bishop's Brothels*) charts the history of prostitution on **Bankside**.

CADE, Jack: (d. 1450). Leader of a celebrated uprising by the Men of Kent. The rebels entered Southwark on 1 July 1450, establishing their headquarters at 'The White Hart', one of the **Borough**'s celebrated **inns**. In **Shakespeare**'s *Henry VI Part Two*, a messenger warns the king:

> Jack Cade hath almost gotten London Bridge;
> The citizens fly and forsake their houses;
> The rascal people, thirsting after prey,
> Join with the traitor; and they jointly swear
> To spoil the city and your royal court.

London Bridge was torched in a nightlong battle. Henry retreated to Kenilworth, as Cade's **mob**, swelled by prisoners released from the **Marshalsea**, proceeded to dispense their own summary justice. The heads of their victims were paraded on poles and made to kiss each other. A Peace Council was hastily convened at **St Margaret's** Church, where a general amnesty was offered. Shakespeare has Jack Cade raging at his deserting army: "Hath my sword therefore broke through London gates, that you should leave me at the White Hart in Southwark?" On 13 July his naked corpse was identified by the landlady of 'The White Hart'. It was beheaded, quartered and dragged through the streets of Southwark. The head was impaled on a spike at **Traitor's Gate**.

CAMBERWELL: Ancient parish to the south of the old **Borough**, encompassing the hamlets of Nunhead, Peckham and **Dulwich**. The village of Camberwell, recorded in the *Domesday Book* as having a seventh-century church, was assimilated into Southwark's southward sprawl. The etymology of "Camber" is obscure. It has been variously suggested that it derives from an old English word meaning jackdaw, or from Cymru (Wales), or that it meant crooked or crippled, and referred to the miraculous powers of its *well* waters to cure the lame. The presence of a church dedicated to St Giles, patron saint of cripples, would seem to support this reading.

CANT: "To use the language of thieves… a hypocritical or affected style of speech." (*Chambers.*) Elizabethan underworld slang, much used by Bankside cony-catchers to conspire in the presence of their unsuspecting "conies". The moral posturing of politicians, as in "cant and humbug".

CANTRIP: "A freak or wilful piece of trickery: a witch's spell." (*Chambers.*)

CARDINAL'S CAP, The: Elizabethan **tavern** and **stew**, scene of **John Taylor**'s showdown with The Globe actors. The hostelry features in his *Travels through more than thirty times twelve signs:*
> We are much better pleas'd with the bare Signe
> Than with the Hat or Card'nale – There's good Wine.

It stood at number 49 Bankside, next door to what is now the Provost's Lodging.

CATHEDRAL YARD: Enclosed churchyard to the south of **Southwark Cathedral**, bounded by Green Dragon Court, where **John Crow** is reputed to have spoken in tongues.

CE: Christian Era. Abbreviation used in this glossary as an alternative to AD (from the Latin, *Anno Domini*: "The Year of Our Lord", meaning after the birth of Christ).

CERIDWEN: Celtic goddess, mentioned in the *Mabinogian.* She is said to have prepared a magic cauldron named "Amen", in order to imbue the ugliest of her three children with arcane knowledge. The village idiot, Gwion Bach, inadvertently drank a few drops of the magic potion. Pursued and devoured by the Mother Goddess, he was reborn as **Taliesin**. The Temple of Ceridwen is believed to have stood on Ludgate Hill. Like St Paul's Cathedral, erected on the same site, it would have been clearly visible from the south bank.

CHARITY: "The check-out girl in **Superdrug**". There is anecdotal evidence that a young black woman by the name of Charity worked in the store during the 1990s, though there is no suggestion that she was acquainted with **John Crow**, or knew that she featured in *The Southwark Mysteries.*

CHARTIST: Britain's Voting Reform Act of 1832 failed to address working class aspirations. A petition in support of a six-point Charter demanding universal suffrage attracted over three million signatures. The delivery of the petition to Parliament was preceded by a huge rally on Kennington Commons in **Lambeth**. Alarmed by this manifestation of people's democracy, the British establishment proceeded to enclose the Commons.

CHAUCER, Geoffrey: (1343–1400.) Poet and chronicler. He is believed to have began work on *The Canterbury Tales* in 1387. The Prologue has his Canterbury pilgrims convening at **The Tabard Inn**:

In Southwerk at the Tabard as I lay
Redy to wenden on my pilgrymage...

It is generally accepted that Chaucer's pilgrims were fictitious, representative medieval types, though the host, **Harry Bailly**, was based on an historical character.

CHRIST: God revealed in the man **Jesus**, the "Word made Flesh". The sacrificial god-king has his roots in pagan fertility cults. His crucifixion and resurrection are prefigured in the Egyptian myth of **Isis** and **Osiris**. To Christians, Jesus Christ embodies God's personal intervention in the human drama, sacrificing himself to atone for the "Sins of the World". Orthodox Christians believe that, in so doing, the son fulfilled the will of God the father. The **Gnostic** Jesus, by contrast, comes to overthrow the false creator god, unlocking the light imprisoned in the darkness. The Southwark Mystery Plays emphasise Christ's love for the world, his unconditional forgiveness of its sins. In his quest to be reunited with his **sakti**, he re-enacts his crucifixion in the foundations of **Winchester Palace**, harrowing hell to reclaim the unshriven souls of **Crossbones**.

CITY, The: Founded by the **Romans**, on the north bank of the Thames, the City has been London's commercial heart since the Middle Ages. The City Fathers denounced **Southwark** as a den of iniquity and a haven for outlaws. Yet it also suited them to have a place of "Liberty and licence" just over the river. By accident or design, Southwark became a dumping ground for things they preferred not to see: **prisons**, **taverns**, **bear-pits**, **theatres** and **stews**.

CLACK-DISH: One of **Master Willie**'s less edifying names for the female part.

CLINK, The: Prison, dating back at least to 1144, when it formed part of **Winchester Palace**. Origin of the expression "in the clink", meaning to be in jail. (See **Liberty of the Clink**.) Over the centuries the prison occupied various locations around **Bankside**, housing whores, heretics and prisoners of conscience, both Catholic and Protestant. It was burned down in the 1780 **Gordon** Riots.

CONSTABLE: Stock character in **Bankside** ballads. This dispenser of rough justice was often portrayed as over-sexed, with cunning plays on his phallic truncheon and on his name, a slang term for the female part, as in this Elizabethan ballad of the press-gang:
> I am a cunning Constable,
> And a bag of warrants I have here,
> To press sufficient men and able,
> At Horncastle to appear:
> But nowadays they're grown so cunning
> That, hearing of this martial strife,
> They all away from hence are running –
> Where I miss the man, I'll press the wife!

The ballad was also sung in Latin, and was called *Astutus Constabularius*.

CONSTABLE, John: (b. 1952.) Presumed author of these works. Southwark poet, playwright and performer, no known relation to the Suffolk painter. In 1986, having travelled widely, in Japan, South East Asia and India, and as a street-performer in Europe, Constable leased an unfurnished attic in **Trinity Church Square**. His plays include *Black Mas* and *The False Hairpiece* (*Sha-Manic Plays*, 1997). He is best known for dramatising Mervyn Peake's *Gormenghast* trilogy and for his solo show **I Was An Alien Sex God**. He claimed to have received *The Southwark Mysteries* from **The Goose**, as mediated by **John Crow**. During 1997–8, he performed the poems in the Southwark Playhouse, the **Clink** Prison Museum, and on 6 November 1998 in **Southwark Cathedral**. By then, *The Vision Books* had inspired the Southwark Cycle of Mystery Plays. Some commentators have argued, intriguingly, that Constable was only a "front", a vulgar pseudonym adopted by John Crow, being one of Shakespeare's 68 synonyms for the female part. (See **Master Willie**.)

CONY-CATCHERS: Con-men, especially cardsharps. In Bankside **cant** their victims were known as "conies" (rabbits).

CORPUS CHRISTI: Latin, meaning "the Body of Christ". The medieval **Mystery Plays** were performed at the feast of Corpus Christi, a celebration of the Eucharist instituted in the thirteenth century.

COSTCUTTERS: Discount food-store, opposite Borough tube station, where **Ali** is said to have worked.

CRACK: Cocaine rendered into a smokable "rock" or crystal state. Its appearance on the streets of London in the early 1990s fuelled a spate of violent muggings, as wired-up "crack-heads" sought to feed their expensive habits.

CROMWELL, Oliver: (1599–1658). Parliamentarian leader in the English Civil War. In 1649 he signed King Charles II's death warrant, establishing himself as Lord Protector.

In *The Southwark Mysteries* he represents the moral law, as embodied in the **Puritans** who shut down the **Bankside** theatres and stews.

CROSSBONES: (or Cross Bones Yard.) Where the whores of the Liberty were buried in unconsecrated ground. According to *The Annals of St Mary Overy*:

> The women... are said not to have been allowed Christian burial unless reconciled to the church before their death and there is an unconsecrated burial ground known as Cross Bones at the corner of Redcross Street, formerly called the Single Woman's burial ground, which is said to have been used for this purpose.

In 1995–6 it was dug up during work on London Underground's **Jubilee** Line extension. 148 skeletons were removed, some dating back to the mid-eighteenth century. It is said that here, on 23 November 1996, **John Crow** met **The Goose**. Some say her bones had been disinterred during the Jubilee Line dig. (See **Halloween of Cross Bones Yard**.)

CROW: "A large bird, generally black, of the genus *Corvus*." (*Chambers*.) **Shaman**'s familiar, as in "the crow on the gargoyle", **John Crow**'s spirit guide in Cathedral Yard. To native American shamans, the crow is a power animal, a shape-shifter with the capacity to learn from the past, live in the present and change the future. The ability to effect magical alterations in the fabric of reality is sometimes referred to as "crow medicine".

CROW, John: Whore's prophet and **shaman**, origin unknown. There is much speculation as to his true identity, or whether he only exists in the vision world. The first reported sightings of John Crow in Southwark were in the autumn of 1996. Some have identified him as a manic depressive ranting in **Cathedral Yard**. (See **Bedlam**.) Others say he was himself a spirit: the wandering soul of a rogue priest who "went native" with the **witches**. There is no historical evidence to support either theory. We should beware of taking *John Crow Trickster* too literally. The poet **John Constable** variously refers to him as an alter ego, spirit guide and shaman's familiar. The Crow's encounter with **The Goose** apparently triggered his emergence as an autonomous entity.

CRUCIFIX LANE: Runs under the railway arches into Druid Street, **Bermondsey**. It takes its name from the Holy Rood of St Saviour, the cross found by the monks of Bermondsey **Abbey**.

DAMIEN HEARSE: Presumably a play on Damien Hirst, the British artist whose dead sheep and cows, floating in tanks of formaldehyde, attracted much controversy. The debate over censorship and death as the "last taboo" was rekindled by the 1998 **body parts** trial at **Southwark Crown Court**. Some art critics speculated that it was only a matter of time before Hirst exhibited a human corpse.

DASHWOOD, Sir Francis: (1708–81). George III's Postmaster General. Founder of the **Hell Fire Club**. When **Sandwich** denounced their fellow rake **John Wilkes** in the House of Lords, Dashwood was heard to remark: "I never thought to hear the Devil preach."

DEKKER, Thomas: (c. 1570–1641). Elizabethan dramatist, prolific author of "low comedies" such as *The Honest Whore*. His plays frequently refer to the Bankside on which they were staged: "The Portuguese will jingle in my pocket like the Bells of St Mary Overie" (*The Shoemaker's Holiday*). He collaborated with Middleton on *The Roaring Girl*, loosely based on the life of **Moll Cutpurse**. He also wrote *The Gull's Handbook*, the tale of a London rake. Despite his prodigious output, Dekker was frequently in debt. He did time in Southwark's Counter **Prison**, and in the **King's Bench** from 1613 to 1616. He died in obscurity.

DICKENS, Charles: Novelist and social reformer. In 1824, his father was imprisoned in **Marshalsea** for a £10 debt. Young Charles moved to nearby Lant Street. Southwark features in many Dickens novels. In *The Pickwick Papers*, the **Guy's** medical student Bob Sawyer lodges in Lant Street, "which sheds a gentle melancholy on the soul." London Bridge was one of Dickens' favourite haunts. David Copperfield sits in its stone recesses watching the world go by. In *Great Expectations*, after Estella's engagement to Drummle, Pip trudges back over the bridge in despair. The old steps down to the river are the setting for the scene in *Oliver Twist* where Nancy betrays Bill Sikes. Sikes' hideout was on **Jacob's Island**, a cholera-infested riverside slum. Dickens was a regular visitor to **The George Inn**, mentioned in *Little Dorrit*. The grinding poverty and brutality of Victorian Southwark helped shape his reforming vision. (See **bridges**, **prisons**, **taverns**.)

DICKENS PARK: Patch of common land to the south-east of **Trinity Church Square**.

DIMETHYLTRYPTAMINE: (or DMT.) Psychoactive chemical, present in **ayahuasca** brews. When smoked it produces a "rush" that is said to transport the user to a parallel universe.

diVinity: The irregular capitalisation in *The OVERIE Cipher* may carry an allusion to Diana, Princess of Wales, killed in a car-crash on 31 August 1997. In her work with people with AIDS. (See **HIV**.) "Princess Di" seemed to invoke the ancient, magical healing touch once used to cure the King's Evil. The myth of divine kingship resurfaced in a welter of conspiracy theories and millenarian cults. In a 1997 video interview conducted by Jeff Merrifield (author of *Damanhur* and *The Perfect Heretics*), a woman calling herself Princess Royale Claire Vittoria Hughes-Capet Habsburg Savoy-Aosta Orleans (*sic*) claims to be Diana's true mother. She produces family trees tracing her lineage back to Christ and **Mary Magdalene**. If the "Princess Royale" is to be believed, then Prince William inherits the *Sang Reale*, not from the House of Windsor, but from Diana, **goddess** of the moon.

DOGS: "Lock-jawed brutality" could refer literally to the dogs bred for bull- and bear-baiting, renowned for the tenacious grip of their jaws. On Southwark estates of the late twentieth century, bull terriers could be seen dangling from their owners' sticks. The reference in *The Book of The Magdalene* is to the Isle of Dogs, bounded by the serpentine coil of the Thames.

DOM: Twentieth-century S&M slang. One who adopts the role of a dominator, as opposed to being **sub**missive. Not to be confused with "Dominator Man", the shamanistic term for the patriarchy that suppressed the female Mysteries. A true master is literally "cruel to be kind", administering pain only to pleasure the slave. **Jahnet de Light**, the living muse of *The Book of The Honest John*, established her reputation as a Mistress (Dominatrix), though she was tantrically submissive, insisting that **John Crow** shaman gained mastery over her before she would bestow her whore's blessing.

DOME, The: Monument to the dawn of a new millennium, erected on toxic wasteland in **Greenwich**. The project was dogged by controversy – over the design and the environmentally suspect materials used in its construction, the cost and, ultimately, the fact that nobody could agree what to put in it. Under pressure from the Church, provision was made for a "Spirit Zone". *A Song of Innocence* refers to plans, announced in 1998, to place the giant replica of a human body inside the Dome. The icon, though symbolically female, had no sexual "part".

DROME, The: Experimental club venue in seven caverns under London Bridge. In 1999 it launched the 24-hour *Warp Experience*. As prophesied, the **Tantric Tribe** returned to reclaim the Liberty, reassembling in Southwark at the dawn of the third millennium. Here **John Crow** performed shamanic raps and rituals, including the second **Halloween of Crossbones**. On 23 November 1999, The Drome hosted *The Goose is Loose* – to celebrate the third anniversary of the raising of **The Goose**'s spirit.

DRAGON: The mythical beast takes many forms, from the red and green dragons of the ancient Celts to the Chinese *lung-mei* or dragon currents. To pagans, the slaying of the dragon represented a vital phase in the cycles of death and rebirth, ensuring the fertility of the earth. Christianity appropriated and reinterpreted the legend in the context of its own moral universe, as in Revelation 12: "And the great dragon was cast down, the old serpent, he that is called the Devil and Satan, the deceiver of the whole world..." The Christianisation of the legend involved building churches on pagan sites associated with dragon-killing heroes. A line of churches, dedicated to the saints **George**, Margaret and **Michael**, stretches across southern England to St Michael's Mount, Cornwall.

DRECK: German, meaning "filth", perhaps imported to Southwark as Yiddish slang.

DULWICH: Ancient manor of Southwark, granted by Edward the Peaceful to one of his Thanes in 967 CE. By the twentieth century it was a relatively affluent suburb, its innate conservatism at odds with the libertarian urban heart of the **Borough**.

DWORKIN, DR: Archetype of the rationalist who denies a spiritual dimension to existence. Perhaps a reference to Richard Dawkins, the neo-Darwinian who took it upon himself to scientifically disprove the existence of God.

ECSTASY: (or MDMA, "E".) A methamphetamine analogue that induces feelings of empathy and euphoria, of being "loved up".

EGYPTIAN: (or gypsy.) Seventeenth-century Bankside **cant**. The gypsies, or Romanies, were popularly believed to have migrated to Europe from India via Egypt. *The Southwark Mysteries* claims them as the source of Bankside's hermetic traditions. They are also identified with the **Tantric Tribe** of which **John Crow** is a self-styled shaman.

EGYPTIAN, The Book of The: Only a fragment remains of the hermetic, missing book of *The Southwark Mysteries*. The legend – that it was dismembered and scattered throughout the other books, and that the task of the adept is to reconstitute it as one of the keys to the Mysteries – echoes the myth of **Isis** reassembling the mutilated corpse of her consort **Osiris**.

EGYPTIAN MYSTERY PLAY, The: Ritual drama, evidently excised from the Southwark Cycle (see Appendix C). The onstage drama is modelled on part of the Moses play from the medieval **York Cycle**, and is chiefly distinguished by The Goose's offstage commentary. Some have suggested it is a decoy, inserted to divert the grasping mind – like the false chambers used to conceal Egyptian temples and tombs from those who seek only to plunder their treasures.

ELEPHANT AND CASTLE: Once famous for its Victorian and Edwardian music halls. By the 1990s it was best known for its roundabouts, which streamed incoming traffic to seven London bridges; its "pink" Elephant shopping centre, where **Charity** worked; and for the Tabernacle, built for the Victorian preacher Charles Haddon Spurgeon.

ELI, ELI, LAMA SABACHTHANI: Hebrew, meaning "My God, my God, why hast thou forsaken me." According to Matthew, the last words spoken by **Jesus** on the cross.

EMPIRE, Roman: The early Christians were a persecuted minority. Many were martyred for refusing to honour the pagan gods of their rulers. In the book of **Revelation**, the Roman Empire is personified as the Great **Whore** of Babylon. Following the Emperor Constantine's conversion, Christians found themselves in positions of privilege and authority. In *Adam, Eve, and the Serpent* (1988), Elaine Pagels charts the shift from a theology of liberation, in which an individual's responsibilities to God transcended any earthly authority, to the establishment of a hierarchical church dictating to the faithful how they should behave and what they should believe. St Augustine's concept of original **sin**, that man's free will had been fatally corrupted by the fall, was cited as proof that humanity was in need of political, moral and spiritual guidance from its appointed leaders. *The Southwark Mysteries* seizes on the paradox that, in the process of converting Rome, Christianity was itself "converted" to an instrument of Empire. The Roman Empire is explored both as historical reality and as the spiritual state that has dominated the Christian era, the contrary of **Liberty**.

ESAU: In Genesis, the son of Isaac, the nomadic "man of the open spaces", cheated out of his birthright by his brother **Jacob**.

ESCHATOLOGY: The aspect of theology concerned with the ultimate destiny of humanity, both in terms of the individual soul and the entire human race. (See **Apocalypse**, **Millennium**.) The phrase "Immanentize the Eschaton" was used by Robert Shea and Robert Anton Wilson in their *Illuminatus* trilogy to evoke the end of the world as the transformation of matter into pure consciousness.

ESTUARY, Thames: Commuter-belt to the east of London. By the end of the second millennium half a million commuters passed through **London Bridge** station every day. In the evening they would "take their trains to **Gravesend**" and other dormitory towns.

EVE: In Judaeo-Christian theology, the mother of mankind, from the Hebrew *Evva*, meaning "life-giver": "And Adam called his wife's name Eve; because she was the mother of all living" (Genesis 3: 20). She allegedly tempted **Adam** to eat of the forbidden fruit of knowledge, thereby bringing sin and death into the world. God specifically punished her with the pain of childbirth, before expelling them both from Eden. The Church Fathers seized on her transgression to emphasise woman's "weakness". The **Gnostics**, by contrast, regarded man and woman as spiritual equals. In their quest for the hidden meanings of Genesis, they turned the story upside down. The *Apocryphon of John* conceives of Eve as Adam's spiritual self, calling out to him: "Arise and remember... and follow your root, which is I, the merciful one... and beware of the deep sleep..."

FLANDERS: During the Middle Ages immigrants settled in **Southwark** and **Bermondsey** to avoid the restrictions on trade imposed by the **City** Guilds. Flemish refugees brought new crafts: **brewing, tanning** and weaving. Weavers would soak their cloth in the Thames and then stretch it "on tenter-hooks" (the origin of the expression). Christ Church Blackfriars, rebuilt in 1960, has 10 stained glass windows depicting local trades of the past and present.

FLY AGARIC: (or *Amanita Muscaria*.) The hallucinogenic red-and-white spotted toadstool of Celtic fairy tales, reputedly ingested by **witches** and **shamans**.

FRITH: Forest. In the York **Mystery Plays**, Mary Magdalene confesses, "I have befowlyd in fryth and fen." The Southwark Cycle transposes the lines to form part of Cromwell's accusation.

GAIA: Greek goddess of the earth, who brought forth life from chaos. In 1979 the British chemist James Lovelock adopted the name for his hypothesis that all life on earth constituted a single, self-regulating, self-evolving living entity. Lovelock speculated that the collective human intelligence functioned as the Gaian nervous system and brain, capable of anticipating and adapting to environmental changes. His ideas, initially ridiculed by many scientists, helped shape the concept of the earth as an integrated ecosystem or biosphere.

GEB: (or Seb.) Egyptian earth god, born locked in a sexual embrace with his sister Nut, the sky goddess. Their myth reverses the convention of sky gods and earth goddesses.

Geb fathered five children by Nut, including **Isis**, **Osiris** and Seth. He was frequently depicted with his sacred animal, the **Goose**, perched on his head. In the Egyptian *Book of the Dead* he is named "The Great Cackler".

GEORGE: Martyr. Patron saint of England. His cult dates back to the fourth century CE and is riddled with conflicting accounts of his life and works. Butler's *Lives of the Saints* suggests that he was martyred in Palestine, probably before the reign of the Emperor Constantine, and that the dragon legend was a twelfth- century accretion. A pamphlet published by St George's Roman Catholic Cathedral, Southwark, portrays him as a Roman soldier put to death by Diocletian for refusing to kill Christians. According to legend, he killed the dragon that was terrorising the city of Sylene, delivering the king's daughter who was about to be sacrificed to it. A variant has him leading the dragon by the maiden's girdle into the city, offering to slay it only if the inhabitants would believe in Jesus Christ and be baptised, a condition to which they, understandably, assented. The legend is an example of medieval Christianity's ability to assimilate pagan sources, in this case the Greek myth of Perseus and Andromeda. It is not known precisely when or how George came to be England's patron saint. Records show that, in 1065, the Minster in **Winchester** possessed a relic of the saint, which failed to protect it from being burnt down on his feast day (23 April). His emblem, a red cross on a white ground, was adopted by crusaders, long before the celebrated "Cry God for Harry, England and Saint George" in **Shakespeare**'s *Henry V.* From the eighteenth century on, St George was increasingly appropriated by nationalist and fascist organisations. The many Southwark place names associated with his legend include **St George's Fields**, the church of **St George the Martyr** and Green Dragon Court, which coils around **Cathedral Yard**.

GEORGE INN, The: London's only surviving galleried coaching-inn, in a courtyard off Borough High Street, adjacent to the former **Tabard** Yard. The timber structure was rebuilt after the 1676 Great Fire of Southwark, though there has been an inn on the site since medieval times. The "Act of Parliament clock" in the taproom recalls the 1797 tax on timepieces. Londoners evaded payment of the tax by ridding themselves of their clocks and watches, relying on church and tavern clocks. 'The George' was one of **Dickens'** favourite inns. He made it the setting for Mr Pickwick's meeting with Sam Weller. The "Southwark Mysteries **Pilgrimage**" traditionally sets off from 'The George'. From 1997–9, the company formed to produce the Southwark Cycle of Mystery Plays held committee meetings in the Talbot Room, which was reputedly haunted. A dark, timbered room at the top of a rickety wooden staircase, it fits Dickens' description of Southwark's "queer old" **inns**.

GLOBE, The: London's first purpose-built **theatre** was erected in Shoreditch in 1576. In 1598 the Burbage family of actor-managers lost their lease on the land. Dismantling the timber frame under cover of darkness, they dragged it over the frozen Thames, reassembled it on Bankside and renamed it The Globe. Many of **Shakespeare**'s plays were first performed here. The theatre burnt down in 1613, when a spark from a cannon fired during a performance of *Henry VIII* set fire to the thatched roof. It was rebuilt with a tiled roof, but was closed by the Puritans in 1642 and demolished two years later. A plaque marks the original site in what is now Park Street. Inspired by the vision of American actor-director Sam Wanamaker, Shakespeare's Globe was reconstructed on Bankside using original materials. It opened in June 1997 with a production of *Henry V*, the play which opened the original Globe.

GLOSSOLALIA: Speaking in tongues.

GNOSTICISM: Mystical tradition which flowered in Egypt in the first and second century CE. Often misrepresented as an early Christian heresy, its teachings proliferated at a time when there was no such thing as orthodox Christianity. As the Church Fathers strove to establish a faith based on a literal reading of selected, canonical Gospels, the Gnostics proclaimed that faith is not enough. Knowledge (*gnosis*) – direct experience of the divine spark within humanity – is the only way to salvation. Gnostic visionaries presented their own subversive improvisations on the Bible stories. In their versions of Genesis, the created universe of matter is inherently evil. The creator god is himself fallen, at best incompetent, at worst downright malevolent. He forbids knowledge to **Adam** and **Eve**, making them serve him in fear and ignorance. The wise serpent is conceived as a precursor of Christ, urging them to remember their own divine origin. There are many variants of a pre-creation myth in which the Divinity creates successive male-female emanations, or Aeons. The *Pistis Sophia* relates how **Sophia**, the Thirteenth Aeon, became entrapped in the material world. The first century heretic, **Simon Magus**, presented his own colourful version of the myth. His association with the whore Helena doubtless helped engender the popular image of the Gnostics as libertines. There is evidence that the Carpocratian sect followed a path akin to that of certain sects of **Tantra**, seeking to exhaust the powers of the flesh by gratifying them to excess. Some of the more bizarre sexual practices attributed to Gnostics, including the "consuming of bodily emissions", may well have been dreamed up by the orthodox Bishop Epiphanius, author of the *Panarion, or Refutation of all the Heresies,* in order to discredit them. The majority of Gnostics lived in ascetic desert communities, seeking to liberate the spirit from the flesh through fasting and sexual abstinence. Their own Gospels (expunged from the Christian Bible by successive Church Councils) claim to contain **Christ**'s esoteric teachings, as revealed to Gnostic initiates. The *Gospel of Thomas* has him talking in **Zen** riddles:

> They said to him: "Shall we then, as children, enter the Kingdom?" Jesus said to them: "When you make the two one, and when you make the inside like the outside and the outside like the inside, and the above like the below, and when you make the male and the female one and the same... then will you enter."

Some texts question the literalness of the crucifixion, arguing that the God in Christ never suffered on the cross and that the resurrection of the body is a blasphemous absurdity. Their Jesus is an angel in phantom flesh, on a mission to liberate spirit from matter, to gather the divine sparks back into himself. In the *Gospel of Seth*, Jesus allows a substitute to be crucified in his place. The *Apocalypse of Peter* conjures a vision of the "laughing Jesus" on the cross. He tells Peter:

> He whom you saw on the tree, glad and laughing, this is the living Jesus. But this one into whose hands and feet they drive nails is his fleshly part, which is the substitute being put to shame, the one who came into being in his likeness. But look at him and me.

In the *Acts of John*, Jesus reveals that he suffers not the literal crucifixion, but the dismemberment of his being in all the parts of creation. The language seems to echo the **Isis-Osiris** myth: "... because not yet has every Limb of him who came down been gathered together... I am not what I am..."

Several Gnostic Gospels allude to Jesus' special relationship with **Mary Magdalene**, to whom he is said to have imparted his "Secret Knowledge". Such ideas were anathema to those seeking to build a hierarchical church founded on faith and the apostolic succession. Following the conversion of the Emperor Constantine, Christianity rapidly adapted to being the religion of the Roman **Empire**. In 325 CE, the Council of Nicea authorised a Christian Creed. As the guardians of an "orthodox" belief-system, the Church Fathers set about eradicating "heresies". In 381 CE the Roman Emperor Theodosius declared that heresy was a crime against the state. Six years later, Christian zealots destroyed an entire Gnostic library at Alexandria. The teachings survived in clandestine copies of apocryphal texts, such as the *Acts of John*, and in the writings of orthodox bishops denouncing them as "abominations". Ironically, Gnosticism's fear and loathing of "The World and The Flesh" was to distort the Church's attitude to sexuality for the best part of two millennia. The pure Gnostic vision resurfaced in the twelfth-century Cathar heresy. The Catholic Church responded with a crusade and an inquisition, complete with public burnings of the heretics. Despite all their efforts, Gnosticism had infiltrated the western hermetic tradition. It spectacularly erupted in the prophetic works of the eighteenth-century poet **William Blake**. During the nineteenth century the *Pistis Sophia* and other Gnostic texts were translated from a few surviving Coptic codices. In 1945, at Nag Hammadi in Upper Egypt, a fourth-century library comprising some 52 Gnostic "books" was discovered in a sealed jar buried in the sand. Their discovery, followed some two years later by the finding of the Dead Sea Scrolls, opened a mystical stream that fed the twentieth-century imagination, from the science fiction writer Philip K. Dick (*VALIS, The Transmigration of Timothy Archer*) to the Goose-Crow poet of *The Southwark Mysteries.*

GODDESS: The divine feminine principle, honoured in *The Southwark Mysteries* as the "female part of God". (See **Brid, Ceridwen, Gaia, Goose, Isis, Kali, Kwan Yin, Mary Magdalene, Overie, Questioning Divinity, Sakti, Sophia, Whore Goddess, Wicca, Yin.**)

GOOSE: Prostitute licensed by the Bishop of **Winchester** to ply her trade within the medieval **Liberty of the Clink**. Hermetic symbol of the Holy Spirit. **John Crow**'s muse and spirit guide, true source of *The Southwark Mysteries.* In *The Book of The Goose* she presents herself as the ghost of a **whore** buried in the unconsecrated **Crossbones** graveyard, whose bones were disinterred in 1996 during work on the **Jubilee** Line Extension. She appears to travel freely in time, claiming intimate knowledge of **Chaucer** and **Shakespeare**. (See **Master Geffrey, Master Willie.**) John Crow honours her as a manifestation of the **Whore Goddess**, reincarnating through history out of compassion for suffering humanity. In the Mystery Plays, she is identified with **Mary Magdalene**, **Isis**, and **Sophia**, the "female part of God". (See **Gnosticism**, **Simon Magus**.)

GOOSE, The Book of The: The first of *The Vision Books* revealed by The Goose to **John Crow**, as transcribed by John **Constable** on the night of 23 November 1996, apparently channelled in a shamanic trance. The vision did not appear from nowhere: the first 57 pages of the poet's notebook are taken up with historical research (including a painstaking transcription of the **Ordinances** relating to the **stews**). On page 58, the neat handwriting gives way to John Crow's spidery scrawl. At page 91, the other voice kicks in, as if he has unwittingly invoked the spirit of The Goose.

GOOSE'S HERESY, The: Hermetic teaching, passed down by Bankside actors and whores, that: "the Magdalene Whore a love child bore..." and that the child was an incarnation of the Goddess of Mercy, her:

> Compassion for all Souls that dwell
> in shadows of mortality
> compelling her to take on very
> flesh of that infirmity
> until she's born a crafty Whore...

&c. thus linking **The Questioning Divinity** of *The Book of The Goose* with the "Magdalene Whore" in *The Book of The Crow*.

GOOSE'S PROPHECY, The: A vision of redemption and healing – the sacred in the profane, the spirit in the flesh. Perhaps mindful of Mother Shipton and others whose prophecies had already passed their expiry dates, The Goose does not reveal the year of her promised **Apocalypse**, though she does mention a specific date, 23 July. The number 23 is associated with violent revelation and transformation.

GORDON, Lord George: (1751–91). Anti-Catholic agitator. On 2 June 1780, he assembled a Protestant **mob** in **St George's Fields** to demand the repeal of the 1776 Catholic Relief Act. Contemporary reports put their numbers as high as fifty thousand. The protest rapidly degenerated into an orgy of burning and looting. Gordon later converted to Judaism, taking the name Abraham George Gordon. He died of a fever in Newgate Prison.

GOY: Jewish term for a Gentile, from *goyim*, often derogatory.

GRAVESEND: Commuter town on the Thames **Estuary**.

GREENWICH: Ancient village to the east of Southwark, bound to the north by the Thames as it curves around the Isle of Dogs. The Greenwich Observatory's contribution to the measurement of space and time is commemorated in the zero meridian that runs through it, and in the internationally recognised Greenwich Mean Time (GMT). The extravagant claim that it was "the birthplace of time" was used to justify its selection as the site for the Millennium **Dome**.

GROPECUNTE LANE: On the old maps, an alley in the City of London. The name suggests that prostitutes were operating within the City walls during the late Saxon period, which ended in 1066.

GUY, Thomas: Born in Horseleydown, **Bermondsey**, the son of a Thames lighterman, Thomas Guy amassed a fortune as a bookseller and by speculating on South Seas shares. As a governor of **St Thomas'**, he used his money to found the world-famous teaching hospital which bears his name.

GUY'S HOSPITAL: Founded in 1726 by **Thomas Guy**. His memorial can be seen in the hospital chapel, along with a plaque commemorating Astley Cooper: "The Undisputed First Surgeon of his Age". (See **Borough Boys**). The reputation of William Lucas, another eminent Guy's surgeon, was besmirched by the activities of his son and namesake, "Billy the Butcher" or "Mad Billy" Lucas. Billy's knowledge of anatomy left much to be desired, a defect reflected in the abnormally high death-rate of his patients. In the reorganisation of the capital's health-care provision during the 1990s, the hospital was threatened with closure. A "Save Guy's" campaign helped win a reprieve, ensuring its survival into the third millennium.

HALLOWEEN OF CROSS BONES YARD, The: Ritual drama, first performed on 31 October 1998 with the actress Di Sherlock in the role of The Goose. The "Goose of Honour", **Jahnet de Light**:

> ... took the spotlight and told us, to righteous, warm applause, about her progress from massage parlour to tantric enlightenment. (Sebastian Faulks, *Evening Standard*, 2 November 1998).

The performance in the Southwark Playhouse was followed by a candlelit procession to the site of the **Crossbones** graveyard, where the dead whores were honoured with candles and precious offerings. The event coincided with a "London Bodies" exhibition featuring a "young woman's syphilitic skull with multiple erosive lesions, from Redcross Way, Southwark, eighteenth century".

> A PLAQUE has mysteriously appeared commemorating the Southwark prostitutes who were buried in unconsecrated, forgotten graves. Playwright John Constable, who has long campaigned for the working women of olde Southwark to be remembered, is delighted. He first spotted the carved wooden plaque on a wall in Redcross Way, Borough, during his performance of a drama honouring the Winchester Geese – the prostitutes employed by the Bishop of Winchester.
>
> (*South London Press*, 6 November 1998)

The plaque, adorned with varnished flowers, was widely believed to be the work of a local working girl named Emily. It read:

> To fix in time, this site the Crossbones Graveyard, where... the Whores and the Paupers of the Southwark Liberty, in graves unconsecrated, lay resting... where now, at Millennial turning, the Whores and the Paupers and our Friends return incarnate, in ritual, with tribute and offerings, to honour, to remember...

HARROWING OF HELL, The: Popular scene in medieval **Mystery Plays**, based on the story of Christ's descent to deliver the lost souls from hell. In *The Southwark Mysteries* **Jesus**' spirit of compassion triumphs over **Satan**'s insistence on the letter of the law. Jesus' judgement, and the responses of the saved and the damned, are based on Matthew 26: 35–45.

HATHOR: Egyptian goddess of love, fertility, dancing and drinking, often confused with **Isis**. She is depicted as a cow, or a woman with the head of a cow. In her destructive, hag aspect, she is Sekhmet the lioness, sent by **Ra** to punish humankind.

HELL-FIRE CLUB, The: Eighteenth-century club for aristocratic rakes, founded by **Sir Francis Dashwood**. In the caves at High Wycombe, his "Mad Monks" are said to have participated in ritual orgies with prostitutes dressed as nuns. Benjamin Franklin, father of the American Revolution, was an honorary member, although there is no evidence to support The Goose's outrageous claim, in the 'Wilkes fragments', that:

Benjamin Franklin,
That Free and Easy Player,
'E finds The Goose at Liberty
And 'e finds the time to lay 'er.
'Tis a little known fact
That the U.S. Constitution
Was conceived by Big Ben
In a House of Prostitution.

The club's most notorious member was **John Wilkes** MP – an inveterate prankster, who once terrified his "brother monk", the Earl of **Sandwich**, by releasing a baboon dressed as Satan in the middle of a Black Mass. The latter reportedly fell to his knees, pleading: "Mercy, Great Devil! I was never half so wicked as I pretended." On 15 November 1763, Sandwich exacted his grotesque revenge in the House of Lords. (See **Wilkes and Liberty**.)

HENBANE: Indigenous British plant of the family *solanaceae*, containing the psychoactive chemicals atropine and scopolamine, reputedly an ingredient of witches' brews. Occult lore has it that **witches** smeared an oil of henbane on their broomsticks, ingesting the drug through the vulva in order to "fly".

HERETIC: There is little historical evidence to support the claim that Southwark was a sanctuary for heretics. Witness the fate, on 10 April 1561, of:

> William Jeffrey, a heretic, whipped at a cart's arse from the Marshalsea in Southwark to Bethlem without Bishop's Gate of London, for that he believed one John More to be Christ, the Saviour of the world. (John Stow, *Memoranda*)

On arrival at Bedlam, the lunatic John More was brought forth and duly proclaimed himself Christ, whereupon he was likewise stripped and "tied at the cart's arse and whipped".

HERITAGE THEME PARK: "London's most historic Borough" was not immune to the sanitised reinvent ion of "ye olde England". **St Mary Overie dock** was graced with a gaudy replica of *The Golden Hind* – though its connection with Sir Francis Drake was tenuous to say the least.

HO: (or Whore.) Twentieth-century slang, frequently used as a term of abuse in the gangsta rap of disenfranchised Afro-Americans.

HORUS: Egyptian god, son of **Isis** and **Osiris**. Following Osiris' murder, Isis hid him in the papyrus swamps of Lower Egypt (*cf.* **Moses** in the bullrushes). Horus lived to avenge his father's death, defeating his uncle Seth in battle, and eventually eclipsed **Ra** as the sun god. He is depicted with the head of a hawk or falcon, or as the child Horus (Greek: *Harpocrates*).

HOSPITALS: (See **Guy's**, **St Thomas'**.) The Goose interprets the presence of two great hospitals within the old **Borough** as a manifestation of spiritual destiny: Southwark is the place of healing.

HIV: The Human Immuno-deficiency Virus, associated with AIDS, the **pox** or plague of the late twentieth century. Unprotected, especially anal, sex and the sharing of needles by intravenous drug-users were the commonest forms of transmission. Fundamentalists, observing the letter of **Levi's Law**, interpreted the disease as a sign of divine retribution. Southwark held fast to the Christian spirit of compassion. (See **Queer**.) Southwark Cathedral houses a chapel of remembrance for "those who live and die under the shadow of HIV and AIDS".

IMAM: Islamic religious leader. In *Twilight of the Trade Marks,* the Priest and the Imam represent fundamentalist Christians and Muslims. Some adherents to monotheistic religions insist that the literal word of God is contained in their holy book, be it Bible or Koran. Others recognise that "The letter killeth. The spirit giveth life", and that "There are many roads to Mecca."

IMMIGRANT AND REFUGEE: Southwark's unique identity was shaped by successive waves of migrations. In medieval times it offered sanctuary to those fleeing religious persecution on the Continent. (See **Flanders**.) Eighteenth-century Irish "navigators" drained the marshes around **St George's Fields**. The Afro-Caribbeans, Indians and others arriving in the decade following the Second World War were not immigrants, but British subjects migrating to the "Mother Country". They came at the invitation of British politicians, including Enoch Powell, whose "rivers of blood" speech fanned the flames of the racism to which they were regularly subjected. Of some five hundred Caribbeans arriving on the *Windrush,* which docked at Tilbury on 22 June 1948, many spent their first night in Southwark. Some settled here, raising new generations that adapted to south London life without losing touch with their roots. In the latter half of the twentieth century they were joined by diverse peoples from West Africa, Latin America and the Far East. The Goose celebrates Southwark's multicultural heritage, whilst acknowledging its "brute ugly face of tribal bile and bigotry".

IMPERIAL WAR MUSEUM, The: Museum dedicated to the history of warfare, on the site of a former **Bedlam** at St George's Circus. In the summer of 1996, Buddhist priests set up a peace camp in the grounds (Geraldine Harmsworth Park). Their rituals included the creation of an intricate sand mandala. Once completed, the mandala was destroyed as a symbol of impermanence. On 13 May 1999, a peace garden was opened and blessed by His Holiness the Dalai Lama, revered by many as a living incarnation of compassion.

INNS: In the days when **London Bridge** was the only bridge over the Thames, travellers would cross over from the **City** before the drawbridge was raised, spending the night in Southwark in order to set off at dawn. **Chaucer**'s *Canterbury Tales* begins at **The Tabard Inn**, the "Pilgrim's Inn" of *The Southwark Mysteries*. At the height of the 1450 rebellion, a headless corpse was dragged through the streets to **Jack Cade**'s headquarters at 'The White Hart'. **Dickens** evokes the inns of Southwark as "queer old places… with galleries and staircases, wide enough and antiquated enough to furnish materials for a hundred ghost stories." He was a regular at **The George Inn**, now the only galleried inn in London. The other coaching-inns are long gone, but have left their imprint in the tall archways and narrow "yards" leading off Borough High Street. (See **Ale-houses, Taverns**.)

IN SHA' ALLAH: "God willing", a phrase frequently used by Muslims to qualify a stated intention. In *The Southwark Mysteries* **Jesus** uses the word to emphasise that **Ali**, his good Samaritan, is not a Christian.

ISIS: Egyptian goddess, daughter of **Geb** and Nut, sister and consort of **Osiris**, mother of **Horus**. In *The Southwark Mysteries*, she is invoked as the goddess of sexual healing and rebirth. "And in me the Broken Man shall be made whole" recalls the myth of Osiris, murdered by his brother Seth. Isis retrieved his body and breathed enough life into it to erect his penis. Fluttering above him in the form of a bird, she received his seed and conceived their child Horus. Knowing that Seth would stop at nothing to kill Horus, she took flight, and was forced to beg in order to support the child. When Seth discovered where she'd hidden Osiris' body, he chopped it into pieces, believing that this would prevent the god's resurrection. Isis wandered the earth in search of his scattered **body parts**, painstakingly bandaging them back together. Unable to find his penis, which had been swallowed by a fish, she moulded him a replacement phallus. Finally, with the help of the Eye of Horus, Isis brought her beloved back from the dead. A **Roman** artefact, a pottery jug unearthed in Southwark and dated c. 100 CE, bears the inscription:

Londini Ad Fanum Isidis
In London, at the Temple of Isis.

Burford locates this temple on the site of **Southwark Cathedral**, formerly the Church of **St Mary Overie**. His theory, propounded in *The Bishop's Brothels*, that Roman prostitutes were initiates of a cult of Isis, was supposedly "affirmed" by The Goose to **John Crow** in a vision.

I WAS AN ALIEN SEX GOD: Dramatic monologue, first performed by **John Constable** at the 1995 Edinburgh Festival, in which **John Crow** makes his first appearance as the author's shamanic alter ego. Only after his encounter with The Goose did he emerge as an autonomous entity.

JACOB: Son of Isaac. The "tent-dweller" who cheated his brother **Esau**, "the hairy man of the open spaces", out of his birthright (Genesis 2: 5). Their sibling rivalry personifies the archetypal conflict between settlers and nomads (*cf. The False Hairpiece*, in *Sha-Manic Plays* by **John Constable**).

JACOB'S ISLAND: Victorian riverside slum, built around a dried-up outlet of the **Neckinger** and regularly inundated at high tide. It is here that the murderer Bill Sikes is hunted down in **Dickens**' *Oliver Twist*:

> Beyond Dockhead, in the borough of Southwark, stands Jacob's Island, surrounded by a muddy ditch, six or eight feet deep and fifteen or twenty feet wide when the tide is in... It is a creek or inlet from the Thames and can always be filled at high water... Crazy wooden galleries common to the backs of half-a-dozen houses, with holes from which to look at the slime beneath; windows broken and patched, with poles thrust out, on which to dry the linen that is never there; rooms so small, so filthy, so confined, that the air would seem too tainted even for the dirt and squalor which they shelter; wooden chambers thrusting themselves out above the mud, and threatening to fall into it – as some have done; dirt-besmeared walls and decaying foundations; every repulsive lineament of poverty, every loathsome indication of filth, rot and garbage; all these ornament the banks of Folly ditch.

JAH NET: "The One Made Many." Not a god*head*, but a network of divine energies invoked to "re-route" the shaman's map of reality.

JAHNET de LIGHT: John Crow's priestess in *The Book of The Honest John*. The daughter of a Scottish whore and an Indian client, she progressed from working as a prostitute in saunas to become a Mistress (**Dom**inatrix), then a **Tantric** sex worker. She met J.C. at the 1998 **SFC** symposium, and was his "Goose of Honour" at the **Halloween of Cross Bones Yard**. They reputedly performed the "Rites of the **Tantric Tribe**" at the SFC beach-party in Hastings and hosted a "Snake Pit" at the Arcadia III party. The account of their work in *The Book of The Honest John* should not be taken too literally. Its explicit sexual imagery, replete with heretical allusions to Christ and Mary Magdalene, is used to evoke mystical states of grace. It can also be read as an answer to **Thomas Dekker**'s scurrilous attack on the **whore** in *The Honest Whore*, which featured in Shakespeare's Globe's 1998 season.

JESUS: "The Nazarene". Jewish mystic, teacher and healer, believed by his followers to be **Christ** the son of God. Strange portents are said to have attended his birth in Bethlehem (*c.* 4 BCE). Rumours of a new-born "king" incited the paranoid King Herod to order the massacre of all male infants. Jesus' **Mother Mary** and Joseph fled with the child into Egypt. Picking up the story 29 years later, the canonical Gospels cover the four years of his ministry leading up to his crucifixion and resurrection. The hermetic tradition suggests that, during his "missing years", he was initiated into the Rites of Isis by **Mary Magdalene**, a high priestess of Egypt.

JEW: A descendant of the ancient tribes of Israel, strictly of the tribe of Judah. A follower of Judaism. The Hebrew Bible charts the conflict between settlers and nomadic tribes, personified in the stories of Cain and Abel, **Jacob** and **Esau** &c. The Jews endured captivity and exile before establishing their own state in Palestine in the sixth century BCE. From its destruction in the first century CE through to the twentieth-century creation of the state of Israel, the Jewish diaspora retained a remarkable cultural cohesion. There is evidence of Jewish settlement in Southwark, including "Yevan Wallchman and wife Isabella" listed, with "Richard Bailif and wife Margery", among the earliest recorded Southwark **stewholders**. In medieval England, Jews were forced to wear badges. They were expelled in 1290. The **Mystery Plays** reviled them as Christ's murderers, glossing over the fact that **Jesus** was himself a Jew. An estimated six million Jews died in the Nazi holocaust.

JOHN: A **whore**'s client. Twentieth-century slang.

JOHN CROW: See **Crow, John**.

JUBILEE LINE EXTENSION PROJECT: During the 1990s, London Underground commenced work on the extension of the Jubilee Line to Stratford via Southwark and Greenwich. An archaeological dig conducted by the Museum of London uncovered a Roman shopping arcade on the upper reaches of Borough High Street, with the remains of a blacksmith's forge, butcher's and baker's shops – along with oil-lamps, bottles, beakers, pottery and bone jars, brooches and ancient coins. The dating of a layer of fire debris confirmed that Southwark was torched by Boudica in 61 CE, along with the rest of London. A mosaic floor discovered under the railway arches suggested the house of a wealthy patrician family. Beneath the old **Crossbones** graveyard on Redcross Way was a large stone building with painted walls. One painting depicted a bearded man holding the head of a sheep – perhaps a priest preparing an animal sacrifice. Most significant of all, so far as *The Southwark Mysteries* are concerned, was the discovery of 148 skeletons of paupers and prostitutes buried in the unconsecrated graveyard. (See **Goose**.)

JUDAS ISCARIOT: The Apostle who betrayed Jesus to the Jewish authorities, allegedly for "thirty pieces of silver". Medieval artists, including the authors of the **Mystery Plays**, graphically depicted the eternal torments in store for him. A roof boss in **Southwark Cathedral** is carved with an image of him being swallowed by the devil. In the new Southwark Cycle of Mystery Plays, Jesus ultimately forgives and releases him. The heretical teaching that Judas was complicit in Christ's mission – that, without his "betrayal", Christ could not have redeemed Man – is contained in the **Gnostic** *Gospel of Judas.*

JUNKIE: Addict, especially of heroin. Twentieth-century slang.

K: See **Ketamine**.

KALI: Hindu goddess of destruction, the hag aspect of **Siva**'s **sakti**. Hindu iconography depicts her with a necklace of skulls and many arms clutching swords and human heads, dancing on Siva's corpse. Dismembered limbs and skeletons litter the blood-red earth; the sky itself is engorged. To the Christian, unable to reconcile the contraries inherent in a dualistic universe, she is, self-evidently, demonic. Her devotees worship her as a liberator, armed with the sword of truth to cut through the veil of maya, the great illusion that divides humankind from its own divinity. She may appear to trample on Siva's dead body. On closer inspection, the god is only sleeping. He smiles, dreaming her dance.

kateEkaos: Katharine Nicholls (b. 1955). **John Constable**'s partner in the 1990s. She stage-managed **I Was An Alien Sex God** and **The Halloween of Cross Bones Yard**, and published *The Book of The Goose* in two "Handmaid by Rough Trade" limited editions.

KEATS, John: (1795–1821.) Poet. As a student at **St Thomas'** and **Guy**'s medical school, Keats lived in Dean (now Stainer) Street, Southwark, and it was here that he composed *O Solitude*, the poem that made his name. His student nickname, "the little pugilist", gives the lie to the popular image of a sickly romantic poet, which presumably dates from the time when he was dying of tuberculosis.

KETAMINE: Anaesthetic, popularised by Dr John Lilly as an aid to inner exploration. Many users reported "out of body" or "near-death" experiences. The drug is generally injected into a muscle. Certain twentieth-century shamans are reputed to have used ketamine to access the **astral plane**, in order to effect changes in the **Akashic Records**.

KING'S BENCH, The: Prison, occupying various sites around Borough High Street, one of the Southwark jails where, according to **John Taylor** the Water Poet:
> ...some do willingly make their abode
> Because they cannot live so well abroad.

For men of means, cells could be furnished and supplied with wine, women and song. During his spell in the King's Bench, John Wilkes entertained the rebel American colonists, who brought him hogsheads of tobacco. (See **Wilkes and Liberty**.)

KUNDALINI: In **Tantra** and other esoteric traditions, the serpent energy that lies at the base of the seven chakras.

KWAN YIN: (or Kuan Yin, Kannon.) Chinese folk deity, venerated throughout the East as the Goddess of Mercy. Her cult is not confined to any particular belief-system. Fishermen worship her as a fertility goddess. To Mahayana Buddhists she is the Bodhisattva who refuses to enter Nirvana until all beings are free from suffering. The embodiment of compassion, she manifests in Southwark "by the Grace of Our Lady Mary Overie".

LAMBETH: London borough, to the west of Southwark. Until the eighteenth century, much of Lambeth was marsh and common land. By the nineteenth century, its overcrowded, disease-ridden slums had nurtured a radical tradition to rival Southwark's own. John Wesley, the founder of Methodism, and **Robert Wedderburn** both preached in Kennington Commons, scene of the 1848 **Chartist** rally. The reference in **The Goose's Prophecy** ("Lambeth below her") conjures an image of Southwark and Lambeth in sexual congress, with the woman on top. *The Southwark Mysteries* are thus linked with older sacred remappings of the world, including those of **William Blake**, who lived seven years in Hercules Buildings, Lambeth. In Blake's prophetic works, London parishes embody spiritual states.

LAWRENCE, Stephen: (1974–93). Black teenager, murdered in Eltham, south London, on 22 April 1993. Five white racists were belatedly investigated and arrested, but the Crown Prosecution Service ruled there was "insufficient evidence" to prosecute. Six years later, an inquiry concluded that "institutional racism" was a factor in the bungled police investigation.

LAZARUS: Brother of **Mary "Magdalene"** and **Martha** of Bethany, whom Christ raised from the dead, prefiguring his own death and resurrection. The *Lazarus* play in the Southwark Cycle, including Lazarus' gruesome account of bodily decay, was modelled on one of the **Mystery Plays** in the medieval Wakefield (Towneley) Cycle.

LEVI'S LAW: Leviticus, the third book of **Moses** in the Hebrew Bible, consists almost entirely of legislation. Chapter 18 deals specifically with sexual morality and "unnatural lusts". Verse 22 says: "Thou shalt not lie with mankind, as with womankind: it is abomination" and was frequently invoked by fundamentalist Christians to justify their homophobia. (See **Queer**.)

LIBERTY: The "name" at the heart of the **Mystery**, the spiritual state wherein the "wounds of history" are healed to give birth to the future.

LIBERTY CAP: The indigenous British "magic mushroom", containing the hallucinogen psilocybin.

LIBERTY OF THE CLINK, The: One of Southwark's five great medieval Manors, or Liberties, extending westwards from the **Clink** Prison to Paris Garden, and bounded to the south and east by King's and Guildable. The fifth manor, Great Liberty, faced east from London Bridge, a C-shaped swathe of land embracing Tooley Street to the north and sweeping south along the **Old Kent Road**. The Clink Liberty was administered by the Bishop of **Winchester** as a quasi-autonomous zone in which the laws of the **City** did not apply. In 1327, King Edward III granted the Guildable manor to the City of London: "that it cease to be a haven for criminals." Southwark's lawless manors were gradually incorporated, but the **Borough** retained its peculiar identity as the **Ward Without**.

LIMEHOUSE REACH: Stretch of the **Thames**, downstream of **Bermondsey** and Rotherhithe, where the river coils like a serpent round the Isle of Dogs.

LONDON BRIDGE: London's first and, until the eighteenth century, only bridge over the Thames. It was originally built of wood and regularly destroyed by fire and flood. In 1014, King (later St.) **Olave** of Norway attacked the Danes who had fortified it. He floated a barge under the bridge, tied cables to the piles and rowed downstream, dragging the supports down and pitching the Danish army into the river. This was the origin of the nursery rhyme, "London Bridge is falling down." The first stone bridge was built at the end of the twelfth century, with shops and houses suspended over the river. Its 19 arches restricted the flow of water, creating strong currents: **John Taylor** the Water Poet wrote of "shooting the rapids under London Bridge". In *The Book of The Goose*, the twentieth-century commuters who "flood back cross London Bridge" create a living contraflow to the crowds of the dead flooding into the City in T. S. Eliot's *The Waste Land*. In 1967, the old Victorian bridge was dismantled and re-erected in Arizona, USA.

LONDON DUNGEON: Museum of torture, execution and other horrors, situated under the arches of **London Bridge** station on **Tooley Street**. Coincidentally, the venue for the first 'Sex Maniac's Ball'. (See **SFC**.)

LOST RIVERS: Until Victorian times, much of **Southwark** was marshland, threaded with some two hundred rivers, streams and ditches. The huge population-increase reduced them to sewers. They were bricked up and forgotten, except in local lore. (See **Blackfriars Ditch**, **Neckinger**.) They symbolise Southwark's buried "Secret History".

LYSERGIC ACID DIETHYLAMIDE: (or LSD 25, "acid".) Psychoactive chemical discovered by Dr Albert Hoffman in 1943. In **I Was An Alien Sex God**, **John Constable** relives his first acid trip in the summer of 1969:

> I step into the field and suddenly Time Is Dead. There's just this one moment and it's like a doorway, and as I step, a hundred blades of grass quiver and bend, a thousand insects scatter, a milliard dancing molecules, as this tiny microcosm of a human step flows into the vastness of this Welsh valley, that dog barking far away – a single integrated event, complete in itself. A moment in Eternity...

The specific, adjectival, use of lysergic could refer to clubbers at the **Ministry of Sound** (though, by the 1990s, **ecstasy** was the drug of choice) or to the **Clink** Street acid house parties of the late 1980s. In her eagerness to embrace a new generation of outlaws, The Goose goes out of her way to show she's not too old to party.

MAD MAUD: In a seventeenth-century "Bedlamite" ballad, the mad lover of **Tom o' Bedlam** sings:

To Find my Tom o' Bedlam,
Ten Thousand Years I'll Travel.
Mad Maudlin goes with dirty toes
For to save her shoes from gravel.
And I will sing bonny boys, bonny mad boys,
Bedlam boys are bonny,
For they all go bare and they live on the air,
And they want no drink nor money.

Tom and Maud's names derive from the names of London asylums. The Magdalene (Maudlin or Maudelyn) Hospital was the female counterpart to **Bedlam**.

MAGDALENE WHORE, The: See **Mary Magdalene**.

MAG WITCH: This could be taken as an allusion to Magwich, the criminal benefactor in **Dickens'** *Great Expectations*. The etymology suggests otherwise. "Mag" is old English slang for a ha'penny. "Mag Witch" may have been a derogatory term used by the Southwark Geese to insult the **Shoreditch** competition. In its hermetic usage, the word refers to **Mary Magdalene**.

MARCHIONESS, The: Thames pleasure-boat. It was struck by a dredger and sank near **London Bridge** on the night of 20 August 1989. Many of the party-goers aboard were drowned. Ten years on, their memorial in **Southwark Cathedral** was regularly adorned with white lilies.

MARGARET'S FAIR: The Southwark Fair, also known as the Lady Fair, was established by Royal Charter granted by Edward IV in 1462. It was held once a year on **St Margaret's Hill** on the 7–9 September. People came from miles around to trade their wares, and the event attracted strolling players and mountebanks. It was also, inevitably, the haunt of prostitutes and pickpockets. Samuel Pepys noted that, when visiting the fair, he always took the precaution of leaving his purse with a local innkeeper. Following a riot in 1743, it was moved to Mint Street, and in 1762, after 300 turbulent years, it was banned as an affront to the dignity of London. Its fruit and vegetable stalls were relocated to Borough Market, which survived into the third millennium. Local pubs were granted special licences to open at 6 a.m. for the market traders, who continued to deal in bushels and pecks.

MARSHALSEA, The: Prison. In 1374, King Edward III required:

> ...the good men of Southwark to build in our Royal Street which extends from the Church of the Blessed Margaret towards the South a certain House for the safe custody of the prisoners of the Marshalsea.

The name derives from an ancient court convened by the Knights Marshal of the king's household, which travelled with the king and exercised jurisdiction within a 12-mile radius of wherever he spent the night. **Wat** Tyler's Poll Tax rebels stormed the Marshalsea prison in 1381, releasing the prisoners. **Jack Cade**'s men did likewise in 1450. During the reign of Queen Mary, the Roman Catholic Bishop of London incarcerated many Protestants in an underground dungeon known as "Bonner's Coal Hole". Following the accession of Elizabeth I, Bishop Bonner was himself imprisoned here. A century later, Wesley records in his *Journals*:

> Feb. 3, 1753. I visited one in the Marshalsea Prison, a nursery of all manner of wickedness. Oh shame to men that there should be such a place, such a picture of hell upon earth!

In 1824, **Dickens**' father was imprisoned here for a £10 debt. In *Little Dorrit*, the eponymous heroine lives with her father in the Marshalsea.

MARTHA: Saint, sister of **Lazarus** and Mary of Bethany, reproved by **Jesus** for complaining that Mary didn't help with the cooking. In medieval Provençal legend, she tamed a **dragon**, binding it with her girdle to lead it into the town of Arles. *The Mystery of George and Martha* contrasts her feminine wiles, integrating the dragon's primordial energy into the human psyche, with St George's act of butchery. Her part in the feminisation of **George** and the healing of the dragon may involve a play on the Gay use of "Martha" – to connote a man adopting a "female" sexual role.

MARY MAGDALENE: First-century saint, to whom the risen **Christ** appears in the garden of Gethsemane. "By the Holy Spirit is Magdalene made Apostle of the apostles" (St Augustine). Luke introduces her as the follower of Jesus "out of whom he had cast seven devils", implying that he cured her of epilepsy or a bi-polar condition. The early church conflated her with Mary of Bethany, sister of **Martha** and **Lazarus**, who anointed Christ's feet (John 12), and with the unidentified sinner who anointed him in the house of Simon the Pharisee: "Her sins, which are many, are forgiven; for she loved much…" (Luke 7). In 591 CE, Pope Gregory the Great pronounced that the three women were one and the same. In *The Women Around Jesus*, Elisabeth Moltmann-Wendel shows how the Church's embellished, composite image of the penitent whore effectively obscured the Magdalene's true significance as a wise woman, healer, and priestess. The Gospel of Luke acknowledges that the disciples found it hard to accept that a woman had been chosen to witness the resurrection. The **Gnostic** *Gospel of Mary Magdalene* points up the implied tensions between Mary Magdalene and the male disciples. In the *Pistis Sophia*, she dominates the conversation with Jesus, prompting **Peter** to complain that no-one else can get a word in. Jesus praises her for elucidating the Mystery of **Sophia**, honouring her as the divine female incarnate. According to the *Gospel of Philip*:

> Christ loved her more than all the disciples and often used to kiss her on the mouth. The other disciples were jealous. They said: 'Why do you love her more than us?'

Philip calls her "The Consort of the Saviour", and reports Christ's promise that she will be reunited with him "in the

Bridal Chamber". She is identified with the bride seeking the bridegroom in *The Song of Songs*, and is named as one of the principal questioners in the *Dialogue of the Saviour.*

> Mary said: "Tell me, Lord, why am I come to this place, for profit or loss?" The Lord answered: "You reveal the abundance of The Revealer."

Her cult flourished in medieval times. She was a popular character in morality and **Mystery Plays**. A legend arose that, in the years after the crucifixion, she, Martha and Lazarus preached in Provence. **The Goose's Heresy** recalls the profane legend that Jesus did not die on the cross, but escaped to France or Cornwall, and subsequently fathered children by her. In this hermetic tradition, the Holy Grail is a symbol of the *Sang Real* or Blood Royal, by which the kings of the French Merovingian Dynasty claimed to rule by divine right, tracing their bloodline back to Christ and the Magdalene. (See **diVinity**.) In the Southwark Mystery Plays, she is honoured as Christ's **sakti**, the embodiment of his love for the world, and as **Isis**, anointing and binding the body of the dead god. Her identification with Egypt may hark back to the legend that **Jesus** was initiated into the Rites of Isis during his "missing years". She gave her name to a church and an ancient parish in **Bermondsey**, and, throughout Europe, to refuges for reformed prostitutes and female asylums. (See **Mad Maud**.) Her feast day is 22 July.

MARY MOTHER: The virgin birth of a god-man has its antecedents in Greek, Egyptian and Oriental mythology. In his account of **Jesus'** conception, Matthew drew on Isaiah's prophecy in the Septuagint Bible. The cult of the Virgin Mary may be founded on the translation of the Hebrew word *almah* (signifying the "nubile" girl who would give birth to the Saviour) into the Greek *parthenos*, meaning a "physically intact" virgin. Over the next two thousand years, the Roman Catholic Church elaborated her legend. At the Council of Ephesus (431 CE) Mary was named *theotokos*, mother of God. Her "perpetual virginity" became an article of faith in 553 CE, although her own "Immaculate Conception" did not become dogma until 1854. Exactly a century later, Pope Pius XII confirmed her coronation as "Queen of Heaven", a title appropriated from the pagan **goddess** Ishtar. In *Mary Magdalen* (1993), Susan Haskins interprets the elevation of the virgin, displacing **Mary Magdalene** as Christ's spiritual consort, as the Church's attempt to create a substitute Mother Goddess, stripped of her sexuality and subordinate to its male authority.

MARY OVERIE: Apocryphal seventh-century saint. The historian **John Stow** mentions "a house of sisters, founded by a maiden named Mary" to which she bequeathed the "oversight and profits of a cross ferry over the Thames". According to legend, her father, John Overs, a miserly Thames ferryman, faked his own death in the belief that his grieving family would eat less – only to be "mistaken for a ghost and clubbed to death". Mary's fiancé, riding in haste to marry her and claim her inheritance, was killed in a fall from his horse. Interpreting this as a sign from God, she is said to have founded a Bankside convent, in 606 CE, on the site of a Roman temple. In *The Southwark Mysteries*, "Our Lady Mary Overie" is invoked as Bankside's patron saint and assimilated into the archaic cult of the **Goddess**.

MASTER GEFFREY: There is no historical basis for The Goose's claim to have spent the night with **Chaucer** at **The Tabard Inn**, though her account of the pilgrimage to Canterbury has the ring of authenticity. (See **Miller's Wife**.)

MASTER WILLIE: This Goose is too much! Not content with stealing some of the Bard's best lines, she seems determined to add him to her list of literary lays. In *The Book of The Crow*, the phrase "secret place" may have mystical connotations: The Goose initiating "Master Willie" into her Mysteries. It has been suggested that **Shakespeare** was schooled in the occult arts by Queen Elizabeth I's astrologer, Dr John Dee. He was certainly no stranger to the sexual pun – nor, indeed, the **Winchester Geese** – his plays reflecting the earthy vitality of the Elizabethan brothel-district in which they were staged. In *Shakespeare's Bawdy* (1947), Eric Partridge reveals that the Bard employs no less than 68 terms for the female part – including baldrick, clack-dish, constable, coun (and country), nest of spicery, O (as in *Much Ado About 'n O Thing*), Pillicock-hill, secret parts, Venus glove and withered pear – and 45 for the male. Doubtless our author would likewise wish to dignify his Goose's bawdy but, however much he tries to dress her up as a respectable woman, like a nervous fiancé introducing her to his parents, she will keep reverting to whorish behaviour that frankly gives the game away. She's had Chaucer, now Shakespeare – heaven forbid she should get her grubby hands on **Dickens**!

MAUDELYN: (or Mawdelayn, Maudlin.) Medieval variants of **Mary Magdalene**, used in English **Mystery Plays**. The origin of the word meaning "tearful", often applied to sentimental drunks. In Bedlamite ballads, one of **Tom o' Bedlam**'s names for **Mad Maud**:
> With a thought I took for Maudlin
> In a cruse of cockle pottage...

MICHAEL THE ARCHANGEL: Saint. Protector of Christian souls against the wiles of **Satan**. "And there was war in heaven: Michael and his angels fought against the **dragon**..." (Revelation 12: 7).

MILLENNIUM: A measurement of a thousand years, particularly applied to the Christian Era (CE). At the end of the first millennium, Europe was ravaged by plague, famine and war. Many believed they were literally living in the "Last Days" as foretold in the book of **Revelation**, and that the world would end a thousand years after the birth of Christ. The sense of impending doom was heightened by an outbreak of ergotism, a disease caused by a rye fungus closely related to LSD. (See **lysergic**.) Victims suffered slow, agonising deaths, accompanied by terrifying hallucinations. Visions of the damned being tortured and devoured by devils cast their shadow long after the day of judgement had failed to materialise. The medieval **Mystery Plays** climax in the second coming of Christ to judge the quick and the dead. By the end of the second millennium, the fragmentation of religious belief had given rise to conflicting visions of the Last Days. Some fundamentalist Christians put their faith in the "rapture" of nuclear incineration. **Gaia**ns, **witches** and **shamans** proposed an alternative **Apocalypse**, in which the material universe would be transformed, rather than destroyed, by the spirit revealed within it.

MILLER'S WIFE: The Goose appears to confuse the tale with the teller. She claims to be the inspiration for the character of Alison, the errant wife in **Chaucer**'s *Miller's Tale*, whose husband Absalon was not himself a miller. Absalon, the reader will recall, begged a kiss in the dark from Alison, and got more than he bargained for:

He knew full well a woman hath no beard,

Yet something rough and hairy had appeared.

The Miller's Wife stanza links the 'Chaucer fragment' with the first verse of *John Crow's Riddle*: "John he go down *on* History." A slip of the tongue? Or a cunning, punning allusion to the oral tradition?

MINISTER OF MORALS: Our Goose understandably has a few bones to pick with the **Puritans**. Healing the rift between flesh and spirit is at the very heart of her Mysteries. Her ancient adversary worships the false god of moral virtue. In *The Book of The Goose* he manifests as a hypocritical 1990s politician, preaching the virtues of "The Family" whilst helping himself to a bit of "rough trade" on the side.

MINISTRY OF SOUND: Late twentieth-century dance club, in Gaunt Street, near the **Elephant and Castle**. By the end of the millennium it had become a shrine to devotees of dance culture. The "outlaw" club scene had relocated to the nearby **Drome**.

MINT, The: The Duke of Suffolk built a palace across the road from the church of **St George the Martyr**, on the corner of Marshalsea Road and Borough High Street. A royal mint was later established there, giving its name to London's infamous thieves' quarter. In Victorian times, when Charles Booth was conducting his survey of poverty, his researcher was warned by a policeman that anyone who ventured into the Mint would be lucky to come out alive.

MOB, The: (or "The Great Unwashed".) A disaffected rabble or the precursor of people's democracy, depending on one's point of view. For centuries, Southwark was subject to sporadic outbreaks of mob rule. During the 1381 Peasant's Revolt, **Wat** Tyler's turbulent Men of Kent beheaded any Italian who could not pronounce "bread and cheese" with an authentic English accent. Less than a century later, **Jack Cade** instituted his own brief but bloody Reign of Terror. In Georgian times, **John Wilkes'** imprisonment in the **King's Bench** (1768–70) helped stir up a hotbed of dissent. (See **pillory**; **Wilkes and Liberty**.) The mob's espousal of "The Rights of the Free-Born Englishman" frequently degenerated to the "tribal bile and bigotry" of the lynch mob, as witnessed during the anti-Catholic **Gordon** Riots. Yet there was also a strong libertarian streak, coupled with the capacity to humble the mighty. In 1850, when Baron von Haynau, the "Austrian Butcher" or "The Hyena", visited Barclay and Perkin's Southwark brewery, the draymen pelted him with horse-dung. Chased up the street, he hid in a dustbin in the yard of **The George Inn** but was quickly unearthed and subjected to further humiliation, before being rescued by the police and rowed to safety on the north bank. The event is commemorated in a local plaque and a Bankside ballad:

> Turn him out, turn him out, from our side of the Thames.
> Let him go to great Tories and high-titled dames.
> He may walk the West End and parade in his pride,
> But he'll not come back again near The George in Bankside.

Another plaque, at the entrance to the John Harvard library, remembers the people of Southwark and Bermondsey who gathered to resist a 1938 fascist march: "They shall not pass."

MOLL CUTPURSE: (c. 1570–1650). Mary Frith, heroine of the Elizabethan underworld, immortalised in *The Roaring Girl*, a play by **Dekker** and Middleton. Moll herself appeared on stage in other plays and may have been the first professional English actress, performing male roles – in contrast to the common practice of boy actors playing female parts. Offstage, she frequently adopted a male persona, wearing britches and smoking a pipe. In 1612, her enforced penance at St Paul's Cross was recorded by John Chamberlain:

> Moll Cutpurse, a notorious baggage who used to go about in men's apparel... seemed very penitent; but it is since doubted that she was maudlin drunk, being discovered to have tippled of three quarters of sack before she came to her penance.

During the English civil war, she wounded and robbed General Fairfax. Arrested and sentenced to hang, she contrived to bribe her way out of gaol. She also operated as a "fence", a receiver of stolen goods, and is said to have established a school for thieves on the lines of that run by Fagin in **Dickens'** *Oliver Twist.*

MOLLY BOYS: Georgian rent-boys. Eighteenth-century slang, loosely applied to homosexuals and transvestites.

MOSES: Hebrew patriarch and lawgiver, who led the people of Israel out of captivity and subsequently received the ten commandments from God on Mount Sinai. Moses is said to have been found in a basket in the bullrushes by Pharaoh's daughter. In *The Southwark Mysteries*, Moses represents the god of the moral law, abrogated by **Jesus**, but subsequently reinstated by the Christian religion. The **Egyptian Mystery Play** relates the hermetic legend that Moses was trained by the priests of Aten to impose their "One God" on the devotees of the Great Mother, **Hathor**.

MUDRA: Ritual posture assumed by Hindu gods, Buddhas and Bodhisattvas to transmit spiritual states, involving precise alignments of the hands and fingers. In **Tantra**, the cosmic orgasm.

MYSTERIES: The Eleusinian and **Egyptian** Mysteries were initiation rites, doorways into the unknown. The hermetic keys to *The Southwark Mysteries* are said to be contained in *The Vision Books*, which precede both the new cycle of Mystery Plays and the commentaries contained in this glossary.

MYSTERY PLAYS: Medieval pageant dramas, performed by craft guilds at the feast of **Corpus Christi** in the cities of York and Chester. There were also the Wakefield (Towneley) and Coventry ("N-town") Cycles. Each play was staged on its own pageant wagon, and performed as part of a "cycle" at a number of "stations" around the city. Adapting the Bible stories to their own time and place, these Mystery Plays tell the history of God and man from the creation to the last judgement, their proselytising leavened with earthy humour. Christian doctrines were thus superimposed on a pre-Christian Mystery tradition, much as churches were built on pagan shrines. The Southwark Mystery Plays could be seen as an attempt to reconnect Christianity with its roots in the **Mysteries** of Ancient Egypt.

NECKINGER: Subterranean stream, one of the two hundred **lost rivers** of Southwark and Bermondsey. In 1899, Besant described it as "meandering through fields and tenter-grounds" near Bermondsey Abbey, flowing into the Thames at Neckinger Wharf (St Saviour's dock). Its course had apparently been altered by the construction of channels to feed the **Abbey** water mill. Its original outlet cut through **Jacob's Island**, the Dickensian slum that flooded at high tide. The name of the stream apparently derives from the "Devil's Neckinger", a term for the hangman's noose. Like Wapping, over the river, Neckinger Wharf was once an execution dock.

NEW BANKSIDE POWER: The old oil-fired power station on the south bank, facing St Paul's, was "new" in the 1950s. The architect was Sir Giles Gilbert Scott, who also designed the British red telephone box and Waterloo Bridge. More than four million bricks were used in the construction of the brick-clad steel structure with its distinctive, if somewhat sinister, 325-ft high central chimney. It stood empty from 1981 until 1994, when the Tate Gallery acquired an option on the site and set about its conversion. The new Tate Gallery of Modern Art opened in the year 2000.

NEWCOMEN, Elizabeth: (1605–75). Southwark philanthropist. She left the income from her estate, in what is now Newcomen Street, to provide clothing for the poor boys and girls of the parish and "for the teaching of them to reade and write and cast accounts."

NEWINGTON CAUSEWAY: Runs north from the **Elephant and Castle** to Borough High Street, following the route of the **Roman** causeway that carried Stane Street across the marshes.

NIGHTINGALE: Having ministered to the wounded in the Crimean War, Florence Nightingale founded her school of nurses at **St Thomas'** Hospital. The nurses of St Thomas' were popularly known as "Nightingales". Southwark's "black Nightingale", the Jamaican nurse Mary Seacole, also nursed in the Crimea. In 1857, a concert in aid of her work was held at the Royal Surrey Gardens Music Hall, close to the present-day **Walworth** Road.

O: The fifteenth letter of the alphabet. Occult "key to the Mysteries" invoked both in sound and written form. Its significance may lie in its identification with Mary **Overie**, not to mention the female part. (See **Master Willie**.) To the **Zen** Buddhist "O" is Mu, the "No-thing-ness" in which all things appear and then vanish without trace. On prostitutes' cards in London phone-boxes, "O" signifies oral sex.

OLAVE: (or Olaf). (995–1030). Patron saint of Norway. In 1014, as the ally of King Ethelred "the Unready", he sailed up the Thames to launch a successful counter-attack on the Danes who had occupied **London Bridge**. During his time in England, Olave converted to Christianity. In 1016 he became King of Norway, and set about converting his native land by the sword. His brutal methods provoked fierce resistance and in 1029 he fled to Russia, where he was killed in battle. Following his canonisation, a parish and church to the east of London Bridge were named after him. Tooley Street is thought to be a corruption of St Olave's Street.

OLD KENT ROAD: Chaucer's pilgrims set out from **The Tabard Inn** down Kent Lane (now Tabard Street and the Old Kent Road), riding east to Canterbury and Dover. Kentish farmers, who drove their livestock up to market or to **Margaret's Fair**, are commemorated in old pub names like 'The Dun Cow' and 'The Drover's Arms'. There was also a Thomas à Becket pub, famous for its gym where many south London boxers trained. To the south of the Old Kent Road lay some have the most desolate housing estates in Europe. It was rumoured that the Scandinavian architect of one notorious "block", on seeing the monster he had created, committed suicide.

OM: Primal seed-syllable of Hindu and Mahayana Buddhist mantras, loosely corresponding to the Christian Logos: "In the beginning was the Word, and the Word was with God, and the Word was God" (John 1) – apart from the fact that Buddhists don't believe in a godhead.

OM MANI PADME HUM: Tibetan Buddhist mantra: "The jewel in the heart of the lotus." The literal meaning of a mantra is secondary to the act of intoning it, wherein the devotee becomes one with the object of devotion, until subject-object cease to exist. All is One, or No Thing, depending on whether one is Hindu or Buddhist. Tibetans regularly intone the mantra in the course of their daily lives. It is painted on the prayer-stones that mark the high Himalayan tracks.

ORDINANCES: "touching the Government of the Stewholders in Southwark under the direction of the Bishop of Winchester instituted in the Time of Henry II" (1161 CE). The Royal Ordinances were approved by a parliament in Westminster and signed by **Thomas Becket**. Under their 39 Items, the stews of the Liberty were officially licensed and regulated "accordyng to the olde custumes that hath ben usyd and accustomed there oute of tyme of mynde".

> Item, that the wommen that ben at common bordell be seyn every day what they be, an a womman that liveth by hir body to comme and to go (so that she paye hir duete, as olde custume is, that is to say every woke xiiij.*d.* for hir chambre) at alle times shal have fre licence and liberte, withoute any interrupcion of the steweholders.

> Item, if therbe any womman that liveth by hir body... cast any stone, or make any contenance to any man goyng by the way, outher by water or by land, she shal make a fine of iij.*s.* iiij.*d.*

> Item, if any woman of the bordel... drawe any man by his gowne, or bi his hod, or by any other thinge, she shal make a fyne to the lord of xx.*s.*

> Item, if ther be any stueholders wif that draweth any man in to hir hous without his wil, hir husband and she shul ben amercyed to the lord in xl.*s.*

The Ordinances provide an intriguing record of the specific problems faced by the Bishop of **Winchester** in policing his lawless Liberty. One such item, loosely translated, states:

> That no Stewholder shall keep any nun nor any man's wife in his Stew, without informing the authorities in advance, upon pain of a fine of twelve pence.

O'REILLY, Mary: Apocryphal Irish nurse of the "Child at Liberty" in *The Mystery of George and Martha.* Clodagh O'Reilly is reputed to have told **John Constable** the legend of **Martha** and the dragon in the yard of **The George Inn**, in the autumn of 1997.

OSIRIS: Egyptian god of the underworld, murdered and dismembered by his brother Seth. His resurrection, assisted by his consort **Isis**, prefigures the **Christ** myth.

OVER 'ERE: On the south bank of the Thames. A variant of **Overie**.

OVERIE: Archaic; meaning "of the ferry" or "over the river". A secret name of the **Whore Goddess**, linking the Bankside saint, **Mary Overie**, with **Mary Magdalene** and the hermetic cult of **Isis**.

OXO TOWER. Erected on the site of a sixteenth-century Royal Bargehouse, the tower, with its famous magenta OXO sign, has been a Thames landmark since 1930, when the Liebig Extract of Meat Company refurbished a former electricity generating station. By the late 1970s the building was derelict and scheduled for demolition as part of a massive riverfront development. A "Save the OXO Tower" campaign was launched, culminating in its purchase and renovation by Coin Street Community Builders.

PASCHAL LAMB: Sacrificial lamb, eaten at the Jewish Passover. In the Coventry (or "N-town") Cycle of **Mystery Plays, Jesus** identifies with the lamb served at the Last Supper, going to great lengths to explain the symbolic significance of eating his various parts:
> Also the hed with the feet ete xal ye:
> Be the hed ye xal undyr-stand my godhed,
> And be the feet ye xal take myn humanyte.

PATRICK: (c. 390–461). Saint. British-born, he was captured by Irish pirates and sold into slavery. He survived to convert his new-found homeland, becoming Bishop, and later patron saint, of Ireland. According to legend, he banished all snakes from the emerald isle. In *The Southwark Mysteries* he represents the Irish Catholics who settled in the vicinity of **St George's Fields**, whose homes were torched by a Protestant **mob** in the 1780 **Gordon** Riots.

PAUL: (b. Saul of Tarsus; d. c. 65 CE). Christian apostle and saint. As a Jewish persecutor of the early Christians, he participated in the stoning of St Stephen. Following his conversion on the road to Damascus, he became convinced of his mission to bring the Christian faith to the Gentiles. His *Epistles* played a key role in the development of Christian theology, propagating the concept of redemption through faith in **Christ**, whose sacrifice had abrogated the old Jewish law to usher in a new age of the spirit. On the downside, Paul's own sexual confusion informed the Church's abhorrence of the flesh, enabling what **Blake** termed the "Religion of Moral Virtue" to reinvent itself in the guise of Christianity. He seems cut out to be the villain of *The Southwark Mysteries*, the archetypal **Minister of Morals**. Paradoxically, the apostle is only referred to as "beating a pan" as the Tantric Tribe re-enter Southwark.

PETER: Christian apostle and saint (d. c. 60 CE). In the Gospel of Matthew, he acknowledges **Jesus** as "the Christ, the Son of the living God". Jesus replies:

> ...thou art Peter, and upon this rock I will build my church... And I will give unto thee the keys of the kingdom of heaven: and whatsoever thou shalt bind on earth shall be bound in heaven: and whatsoever thou shalt loose on earth shall be loosed in heaven.

At the Last Supper, Jesus challenges Peter's boast that he will never desert him:

> I tell thee, Peter, the cock shall not crow this day, before that thou shalt thrice deny that thou knowest me. (Luke 22:34)

In Christian tradition, Peter is credited as the founder of the Church and its apostolic succession. He is the embodiment of faith and male authority, in opposition to **Mary Magdalene** and her female, visionary path of the Holy Spirit.

PILGRIM: Chaucer's Canterbury pilgrims convened at **The Tabard Inn**. In neighbouring **Bermondsey**, the 'Mayflower' pub stands close to the dock from which the Pilgrim Fathers set sail for America.

PILGRIMAGE: On 14 November 1996 (nine days before his night of visions) the poet **John Constable** conducted a group of actors and writers on a "Southwark Mysteries Pilgrimage".

The pilgrimage was revived for the 1998 Southwark Festival. By the third millennium, it was established as an annual event. Pilgrims traditionally assemble at **The George Inn**, before setting out to trace **John Crow**'s journey through the back-streets of Southwark, honouring the old sacred sites of the **Liberty**.

PILLORY: The public pillory was on **St Margaret's Hill** (Borough High Street). Being pilloried included being pelted with rotten eggs, fruit and ordure, and many did not survive the ordeal. Yet the **mob** was unpredictable. The **printer** of *The North Briton No.45* (see **Wilkes and Liberty**) was borne to his place of punishment in a hackney carriage. The pillory was carefully washed clean for him and not a single egg was thrown. Instead, the mob brought him food and drink and had a whip-round on his behalf, all under the gaze of a nervous king's militia.

PONCE: Pimp. Derogatory term for an effeminate man.

PONTIUS PILATE: Governor of Judaea c. 26–36 CE. When Christ was accused before him, he found "no fault in this man" but infamously "washed his hands", permitting the Crucifixion.

PORK PACKING: Necrophilia. Twentieth-century slang.

PRINTER: Southwark has long been a home to printers and publishers – the title page of Coverdale's first English Bible reads: "Imprinted in Southwarke in Saint Thomas Hospitale by James Nycolson, 1537."

PRISONS: (See **Clink**, **King's Bench**, **Marshalsea**.) In the words of John Taylor the Water Poet:
> Five jails or prisons are in Southwark place,
> The Counter (once St Margaret's Church defaced),
> The Marshalsea, The King's Bench and White Lion...
> Then there's the Clink, where handsome lodgings be...

Not to mention Surrey County and the Sheriff's Prison. The **City** of London kept its houses of correction together with other houses of ill repute over the river in the **Ward Without**. Their presence only served to stir-up The Borough's hotbed of political dissent. The gaols were repeatedly sacked and prisoners released. In 1780, the Clink was torched by the **Gordon** Rioters. (See **Wilkes and Liberty**.) A new gaol was built at Horsemonger Lane where, in 1849, **Dickens** witnessed the public hanging of Mr and Mrs Manning. He wrote to *The Times*:

> I do not believe that any community can prosper where such a scene of horror as was enacted this morning outside the Horsemonger Lane gaol is permitted. The horrors of the gibbet and of the crime which brought the wretched murderers to it faded in my mind before the atrocious looks and language of the assembled spectators.

A 1997 archaeological excavation, of the land between **Trinity Church Square** and the park known locally as "Jail Gardens", unearthed the foundations of Victorian terraced houses. The inhabitants are believed to have rented out rooms to spectators at the Mannings' hanging. Dickens' letter hastened the abolition of this particular form of "entertainment".

POX: Syphilis; the "burning sickness".

> Item, that no stewholder shall keep any woman within his house that hath any sickness of *brennynge*, but that she shall be put out, upon pain of making a fine unto the lord of twenty shillings. (From the Ordinances relating to the stews.)

POX-RIDDEN MAJESTY: The British establishment in general, and Henry VIII in particular – the syphilitic king who shut down the Bankside **stews**. By Elizabeth I's reign, Southwark was firmly re-established as London's pleasure quarter.

PUMP and PADDLE: May refer to the ferrymen rowing clients over the river, or to our Goose's own whorish arts.

PUNK: Prostitute, Elizabethan slang. In 1940s US *film noir*, a small-time hoodlum. In the 1970s young British anarchists adopted the word to flaunt their rejection of social norms.

PURITANS: English Protestant sect which sought to reform the Anglican Church. Their insistence on scriptural authority liberated Christians from Episcopal tyranny, emphasising the individual relationship with God. Yet it also encouraged a fixation on the letter, as opposed to the spirit, of the law. The Puritan Revolution of the 1640s saw the emergence of many radical sects, including the Levellers, who advocated religious freedom and political suffrage. With **Cromwell**'s installation as Lord Protector, the regime became increasingly totalitarian. Following his death in 1658, 'The Commonwealth' collapsed, prompting the restoration of Charles II.

QUEENHITHE: Roman dock, on the north bank of the Thames, facing Bankside. According to **Burford**, it was also a slave-market.

QUEER: Derogatory term for a homosexual. In the 1990s, a service of blessing and penitence for gay and lesbian Christians in **Southwark Cathedral** raised howls of homophobic outrage. The word "queer" was eventually reclaimed by gays, and even adopted by some heterosexuals wishing to escape their own "straight" sexual stereotyping.

QUESTIONING DIVINITY, The: The **Mystery** of the divine taking on flesh out of compassion for suffering humanity carries heretical echoes of Christ: "And the Word was made Flesh" (John 1). In **The Goose's Heresy**, a female divinity incarnates as a "crafty Whore". Buddhists may be reminded of **Kwan Yin**, the Chinese Goddess of Mercy. The Goose could be referring to an archaic cult of the **Goddess**, assimilated into the worship of **St Mary Overie**.

RA: Egyptian sun god, said to have created the universe by masturbating in the holy place of On (ancient Egyptian city of Heliopolis). His children, the god Shu and goddess Tefnut, in turn gave birth to **Geb** and Nut, the parents of **Isis** and **Osiris**. Like the Hebrew creator god, **Yahweh**, Ra sometimes despaired of his creation and sought to destroy it. He sent **Hathor** to scourge the human race but, witnessing her insatiable blood-lust, was forced to intervene to prevent its annihilation. Another legend tells how Isis tricked Ra into revealing his secret name, the source of his power, and granting her the Eye of Ra. Isis gave the Eye to **Horus**, who eventually displaced Ra as the god of the sun.

REDCROSS WAY: Runs north from Marshalsea Road past the site of the **Crossbones** graveyard. Redcross Cottages, with their attractive communal hall and gardens were built by the Victorian philanthropist Octavia Hill. (See **Sisters of Redcross.**)

RENTS: (or yards.) The names of **Bankside**'s medieval alleys – Foul Lane, Pyssynge Alley, Codpiece Lane, Sluts Hole, Whore's Nest &c. – made no attempt to disguise their physical and moral squalor. The anomaly was Maiden Lane, site of the original **Clink** prison, where records show **Stews** dating back to 1251. By the sixteenth century many alleys and yards had adopted the names of the landlords to whom their rents were due – Cordwainer's Rents, Rockett's Rents &c. – though there is no suggestion that these new names improved either the sanitation or the morals. There was also a Love Lane and a Bear Gardens. (See **Bear-baiting.**)

REVELATION, The book of: Apocalyptic last book of the Christian Bible, attributed to "John the Divine". Rooted in the Jewish **apocalypse** tradition, its cataclysmic vision profoundly influenced the medieval obsession with the last judgement. (See **Millennium**). The book of Revelation continues to inspire a welter of conflicting exegesis. Theologians generally agree that the Great **Whore** of Babylon symbolises the

Roman **Empire**, and that the number of the beast, 666, is a cryptogram of Nero Caesar. Pre-millennial conspiracy theorists warned that the number 666 was encrypted in the ubiquitous retail barcode.

> ...that no man might buy or sell, save he that had the mark, or the name of the beast, or the number of his name. (Revelation 13)

ROAST BEEF ON THE BONE: Roast beef was traditionally regarded as a symbol of Englishness. The "Mad Cow Disease" of the 1980s and 1990s, and the consequent banning of beef "on the bone" devastated the national psyche.

ROAST PORK: "and Bacon fat". The Goose's compassion extends to the beasts of the field, as witness her apocalyptic nursery rhyme on the horrors of "factory farming".

ROMAN. Julius Caesar's first and second Roman invasions of Britain (55 and 54 BCE) made little impression on the London area. In 43 CE, the Emperor Claudius returned with an army and a herd of elephants. He established a bridgehead and garrison on the south bank, then no more than a cluster of sandy islands threaded with channels and rivulets. At first, Londinium was a minor speculative settlement, far less important than Colchester or St Albans. In 61 CE the city was razed to the ground by the Iceni tribe, under the command of Queen Boudica, whose daughters had been raped by Roman soldiers. Following Boudica's defeat and suicide, the Romans rebuilt the south bank settlement, with two great roads leading up to **London Bridge**. The **Old Kent Road** and **Newington Causeway** respectively follow the original routes of Watling Street (from Dover) and Stane Street (from Chichester), converging at the church of **St George the Martyr**. By the end of the second century Southwark had a population of more than three thousand. Archaeological excavations conducted by the Museum of London during the 1990s **Jubilee** Line Extension Project uncovered second-century buildings and artefacts, providing important clues to life in Roman times.

Other artefacts, discovered on earlier digs, are displayed in the Cuming Museum, **Walworth Road**. The so-called "**Isis** jug", found on the Thames foreshore in 1912, inspired **E. J. Burford**'s theory that Roman prostitutes worshipped the Goddess at her temple on the site of **Southwark Cathedral**.

RYLANCE, Mark: Actor. First artistic director of the reconstructed Shakespeare's Globe. *The Book of The Constable* names "Rylance and **Slee**" as potential players in a millennial act of healing and renewal.

SAINT: In *The Southwark Mysteries* Christian saints are portrayed as living energies and intelligences, working to transform Southwark's spiritual state. (See **Brid**, **George**, **Margaret**, **Martha**, **Mary Magdalene**, **Olave**, **Paul**, **Peter**, and **Thomas**.) Bankside's own patron saint, **Mary Overie**, does not figure in the Anglican or Roman Catholic calendars. Church historians deny that she ever existed, arguing that the Church of **St Mary Overie** would have been dedicated to Mary Magdalene or the Virgin Mary, and that Overie merely signified "over the river". It seems her cult was driven underground long before the Reformation.

ST GEORGE THE MARTYR: There has been a church at the junction of Borough High Street and the former Kent Lane (now Tabard Street) since the eleventh century. In 1122 it was presented to the **Abbey** of Bermondsey. It was rebuilt in the fourteenth and eighteenth centuries. The foundation stone of the present church was laid on St George's Day, 1734. Repair-work carried out during 1938 uncovered "masses of skulls and bones" under the floor. In 1952, following restoration, the church was rededicated by the Bishop of Southwark. The peal of its bells can be heard all over the Borough. One great bell in the tower originally hung in Horsemonger Lane Gaol, where it tolled the death-knell for convicted criminals. (See **Prisons**.) When **Dickens**' Little Dorrit was locked out of the adjacent **Marshalsea** prison, she spent the night in the vestry, using an old burial register as a pillow. The steeple has four clock faces, only three of which are lit. Local lore has it that they were paid for by public subscription, but that the people of Bermondsey refused to pay for their time. The east-facing clock thus remained dark.

ST GEORGE'S FIELDS: Scene of an infamous "massacre", when George III's militia opened fire on the friends of **Wilkes and Liberty**. As late as the eighteenth century the area around what is now St George's Circus was open marshland crossed by footpaths with names like Dirty Lane and Bandyleg Walk. The original Christ Church on **Blackfriars** Road, erected in 1671, sank up to its windows in mud within fifty years. The Irish Catholics who drained the marshes were forbidden to worship in public. They were forced to congregate in secret Mass-houses, including a slum in Kent Street (now Tabard Street). In 1780, Lord George **Gordon** assembled a Protestant mob in St George's Fields in protest at the Catholic Relief Act. In the ensuing Gordon Riots, Catholics were set upon and their property burnt. The 1848 opening of St George's Roman Catholic Cathedral established a spiritual home for Southwark citizens of Irish and Italian descent. Its present congregation includes Nigerians, Tamils and Mauritians. Across the road is the site of a former **Bedlam**, now the **Imperial War Museum** and Tibetan peace garden. At St George's Circus, an eighteenth-century obelisk marks the distances to Westminster and the City.

ST MARGARET'S: Ancient parish of **Southwark**. The parish church stood just south of **London Bridge**, on **St Margaret's Hill**. By Tudor times it had been turned into the Counter **Prison**. Following the English Reformation, the parish was amalgamated with **St Mary Magdalene's** to create the new parish of **St Saviour's**.

ST MARGARET'S HILL: On the old maps, the name for what is now Borough High Street, running south from **London**

Bridge. From 1462 to 1762 it was the site of the notorious **Margaret's Fair**.

ST MARY MAGDALENE'S: Ancient parish of **Bermondsey**. The parish church of St Mary Magdalene dates from 1291, though it was substantially rebuilt in 1680 and again in 1830. In Tudor times, the neighbouring Southwark parish of St Mary Magdalene's merged with **St Margaret's** to become **St Saviour's**.

ST MARY OVERIE: Medieval church, founded in 1106 by the Priory of St Mary Overie for use by parishioners. It is said to have ministered to a Bankside congregation of **actors** and **whores**. Following the dissolution of the Priory in 1539, it was rededicated to **St Saviour**. (See **Southwark Cathedral**.)

ST MARY OVERIE DOCK: On the south bank of the Thames, between **Southwark Cathedral** and **Winchester Palace**. The ancient dock is mentioned in the *Domesday Book*. Landing fees were divided between the King and the Bishop of Winchester. According to legend, it was the dock of the sixth-century Overie ferry. In 1998, a granite plaque was erected here, relating a variant of the **Mary Overie** story in which John Overs, the miserly ferryman, pretends to have died in bed. Roused by the din of his servants' rejoicing, he jumps out of the coffin, is mistaken for a ghost &c.

ST MARY OVERIED: Etymology uncertain. Bankside slang. (*cf.* "fucked" or "shafted" – though the connotations are more brutal).

ST OLAVE'S: Parish to the east of **London Bridge**, dating back to the eleventh century. The medieval parish had a high proportion of Flemish refugees. (See **Flanders**, **Immigrants**.) The parish church was demolished in 1928.

ST SAVIOUR'S: Southwark parish dating back to the English Reformation, when the parishes of **St Margaret's** and **St Mary Magdalene's** were amalgamated. The parish church of **St Mary Overie** was rededicated to St Saviour (Christ). The name was taken from the dedication of the former Bermondsey **Abbey**, and from its Holy Rood, which was worshipped as the true cross. Following the 1905 creation of the Anglican diocese of Southwark, the parish church became **Southwark Cathedral**.

ST THOMAS A WATERING: On the old maps, the stream crossing Kent (now Tabard) Street, where **Chaucer**'s pilgrims stopped to pray on their pilgrimage to Canterbury. In 1415, the clergy gathered here to honour King Henry V on his return from Agincourt, escorting him in triumphal procession over London Bridge. There was also a public gallows and a hospital for lepers, close to what is now the **Old Kent Road** flyover.

ST THOMAS' HOSPITAL: In 1212 a great fire destroyed London Bridge and the nearby hospital in the Priory of **St Mary Overie**. Hundreds were burned or drowned. The disaster led to the founding of a new hospital named after St **Thomas** Becket. In 1536, Edith Percke was charged with operating a brothel inside the hospital. St Thomas' was shut down during the Reformation, then reopened, rededicated to St Thomas the apostle. Dick Whittington, the Lord Mayor of London commemorated in pantomime and nursery rhyme, is rumoured to have funded a secret ward for "women gone amiss". In Victorian times the hospital maintained "clean" and "foul" (VD) wards. In the nineteenth century it was forced to relocate to Westminster Bridge, to make way for the expansion of London Bridge station. The Old Operating Theatre and Herb Garret has survived as a museum. The former tuberculosis ward is now a post office.

SAKTI: Pronounced "Shakti". The female aspect of a Hindu deity, especially **Siva**, symbolised by the *yoni*, a stylised representation of the female part. Sakti is specifically honoured in the tantric rites of **Siva-Sakti**. The teaching of **Tantra** that, without his sakti, Siva is nothing, is expressed in icons of the hag **Kali** with her necklace of skulls, dancing on Siva's corpse.

SANCTUARY: King Edward the Confessor established the right of outlaws to claim sanctuary in churches. To all intents and purposes, vast tracts of London lay outside the law. Southwark's **Mint** was the last of these *de facto* sanctuaries. When it was finally abolished, thousands marched to the Guildford Quarter Sessions to avail themselves of a blanket amnesty.

SANDWICH, John Montagu, Fourth Earl of: (1718–92). Georgian rake, said to have invented the "sandwich" so as not to have to leave the gaming table at mealtimes. He was also a ruthless seducer of young girls, privately boasting that "the corruption of innocence is in itself my end". In 1763 he orchestrated a show trial in the House of Lords, piously denouncing **John Wilkes** as the author of a "scandalous, obscene and impious" poem. In reality, both men were members of **Sir Francis Dashwood**'s orgiastic **Hell Fire Club**, which was how Sandwich had come by his copy of Wilkes' *Essay On Woman*. His moral posturing prompted the following memorable parliamentary exchange:

> Sandwich: You, sir, will either die on the gallows or of the pox!
>
> Wilkes: That depends, sir, whether I embrace your principles or your Mistress.

In the 'Wilkes fragments', the old hypocrite is mocked and vilified, as in this variant on a well-known nursery rhyme:

> As Lucy Locket I lost my pocket.
> As Kitty Fisher I found it.
> I cut and spread and buttered me Bread
> And danced a jig around it.

> So raise your Cocks to Lucy Locket
> And all the Whores of London,
> But happy the man who has in his pocket
> A stout and sturdy condom.

Kitty Fisher was one of the great courtesans of Georgian London who, as the rhyme implies, became Sandwich's mistress, stealing him from Lucy Locket. Kitty evidently delighted in cuckolding and humiliating her new master. In the Royal Exchange, she called for a £10 note to be placed between two slices of bread and proceeded to eat it. It has been suggested that Sandwich served as a model for The Goose's **Minister of Morals**.

SATAN: The Hebrew-Christian devil. He makes fleeting appearances in the Bible, tormenting Job, and failing to tempt Christ in the wilderness. The legend of the fallen angels derives from three verses in Revelation 12: 7–9. The medieval church embellished the legend, conflating the horned god Pan and other pagan deities to create its supreme embodiment of evil. Satan features prominently in the medieval **Mystery Plays**, a bawdy, scatological, pantomime villain, delighting in his own wickedness. In the Southwark Cycle he is "the Accuser", invoking the moral law to stake his claim to the souls of "sinners".

SEACOLE, Mary: A nurse. (See **Nightingale**.)

SFC: The Sexual Freedom Coalition, a "pansexual" libertarian alliance, founded by porn star and sex therapist Dr Tuppy Owens following the banning of her 'Sex Maniac's Ball'. The SFC's campaign to reform Britain's sex laws was based on two principles: "Consenting Adults. No Coercion." JC reportedly performed *The Book of The Goose* at the SFC's 1998 symposium, where he met **Jahnet de Light**.

SHAKESPEARE, William: (1564–1616). Poet and playwright. Little is known of the man from Stratford-upon-Avon, whose supposed gravestone bears no name. It is generally accepted that a Will Shakespeare, or Shagspur, was one of the eight

Lord Chamberlain's Men who held shares in The Globe. The parish records of **St Saviour's** show that his brother Edmund was buried in what is now **Southwark Cathedral**. It is said he was buried in the morning, so the actors could perform in the afternoon – an example of the time-honoured adage that "the show must go on". Will had evidently made a big impression on London's theatre world by 1592, prompting Robert Greene to parody a line from *Henry VI Part Three* in his vitriolic attack on the young playwright:

> ...there is an upstart crow, beautified with our feathers, that with his *Tyger's hart wrapt in a Players hyde*, supposes he is as well able to bombast out a blanke verse as the best of you: and... is in his own conceit the onely Shake-scene in a countrey...

Some have developed Greene's charge of literary plagiarism, asserting that a butcher's son, a mere jobbing actor or "Spear Shaker", could not have been the author of such sublime works. The plays have been variously claimed as the work of Sir Francis Bacon, the Earl of Oxford and Christopher Marlowe. A pamphlet published by the Francis Bacon Research Trust (1999) suggests that Bacon deliberately concealed his authorship, mirroring the Masonic Mysteries, in which the author of the universal drama remains hidden. In *The Secret Life of The Virgin Queen* (1946), Comyns Beaumont claims to have cracked the ciphers encrypted in the plays, revealing that Bacon was the bastard son of Queen Elizabeth I and that he wrote the plays and sonnets to stake his claim as the rightful heir to the throne.

SHAMANISM: The art of effecting magical alterations in the fabric of reality. Unlike the priest, the shaman does not represent a fixed belief-system. In hunter and gatherer cultures from the Americas to the Himalayas, shamans mediated between the tribe and the vision world. Drumming, dancing, fasting, chanting and sympathetic magic were used to induce states of trance. Despite their key role in the spiritual lives of their communities, shamans were frequently regarded with suspicion, as outsiders. Such men appeared to embrace their outcast status, often assuming comical or grotesque names. (See **Broken Wing John**

Crow.) The word "shaman" is Siberian in origin. Siberian shamans ingested **fly agaric**, embarking on visionary quests, returning with messages from the ancestors, songs, spells and healing ceremonies. In *The Sacred Mushroom and The Cross*, John Allegro employs linguistic analysis of the scriptures to support his proposition that the early Christians were initiates of an hallucinogenic mushroom cult, and that **Christ** is the personification of fly agaric. The red-and-white spotted toadstool and the **Liberty Cap** are both native to Britain, yet there is no evidence of their use prior to the eighteenth century. In *The Southwark Mysteries* **John Crow** is identified as a "chemical shaman". The twentieth-century Western "shamanic" revival was fuelled by experiments with sacramental plants and their synthetic analogues. On 16 April 1943, Dr Albert Hoffman, research chemist at the Sandoz laboratory, Switzerland, accidentally ingested a microscopic amount of **lysergic acid diethylamide** through his fingertip, and was interrupted in his work by "unusual sensations". The rest is history.

SHEND: Middle English, "to destroy." Shent: "destroyed".

SHEPPARD, Jack: (1702–1724). Outlaw. Captured five times. Escaped four times from prison. He took refuge in the **Mint**, but was eventually arrested and sentenced to death. His execution at Tyburn, on 16 November 1724, was followed by a riot over the disposal of the corpse.

SHOREDITCH: Parish to the north of the City of London. Home to London's first purpose-built **theatre**, which was dismantled and relocated to **Bankside** in 1598. (See **Globe**.) The rivalry between the north and south bank pleasure-quarters is made explicit in one of the 'Wilkes fragments':

Now yer hot bitch from Shoreditch –
O don't look so offended, dear –
Whatever they do Over There
We do it better Over 'ere.

SHUFFLE: Dance step used by **witches** and **shamans** to exorcise the past, thereby reinventing the present and the future.

SIMON MAGUS: First century **Gnostic**, denounced by the early Church as "the Great Heretic". He reputedly worked with a whore named Helena, whom he had rescued from a brothel in Tyre, and whom he honoured as the divine female emanation, trapped in the created universe of matter:

> ... she was even enclosed in human flesh and migrated for centuries as from vessel to vessel into different female bodies. And since all the powers contended for her possession, strife and warfare raged among the nations wherever she appeared... Migrating from body to body, she at last became a whore in a brothel.

The archetype appears to reinvent itself in the legend of **John Crow** and The Goose.

SIN: The alienation of a creature from God. In the Hebrew Bible, the rift between the human and divine is blamed on the wilful disobedience of **Adam** and **Eve**. This model was adopted and developed by the early Christians. St Augustine advanced the doctrine of original sin, which held that all descendants of Adam were fatally infected with his sin. Though he insisted that the fall was precipitated by pride, not lust, Augustine drew on his own lifelong struggle with sexual incontinence to show how the soul was not in control of its bodily parts and instincts. In so doing he, perhaps unwittingly, laid the foundations for the identification of sexuality with sin, which was to deform Christian theology for the next fifteen hundred years.

SISTERS OF REDCROSS: Apocryphal order of whore-nuns, ministering to those the established church cannot or will not reach. They are said to play key roles in the Healing of **George** and the **dragon** and in the hallowing of **Crossbones** Yard.

SITA: In **Vedic** myth, the consort (**Sakti**) of the god king Rama.

SIVA: Pronounced "Shiva". **Vedic** god of generation, symbolised by the phallic *linga*. J.C. is said to have found a moulded relief of Siva and his **sakti** on the Thames mudflats, which subsequently adorned the bathroom in Trinity Church Square. In the Hindu Trinity – with Brahma the creator and Visnu the preserver – Siva is the destroyer, liberating beings from maya, the veil of illusion.

SIVA-SAKTI: In **Tantra**, consummation of male-female energy in perfect union. The destruction of the ego in surrender to the cosmic dance.

SLEE, Very Rev. Colin: As Provost of **Southwark Cathedral** in the late 1990s, Slee endorsed the creation of a new Southwark Cycle of **Mystery Plays** as part of the Cathedral's millennium celebrations. Having urged **John Constable** to retain the traditional narrative of the medieval Mysteries, he was understandably perturbed by a *Sunday Times* report that, "In the middle ages, mystery plays were based on the Bible, but the pagan Constable is plotting something rather different." Following the performance in the Cathedral on 6 November 1998, he publicly embraced the poet. In September 1999, having read the new Mystery Plays, the Cathedral reaffirmed its support, whilst expressing "certain anxieties" as to "some clear heresies... the name of Christ is associated with other deities..." and "use of the feminine within the Cathedral in relation to the person of God."

SOPHIA: In the Septuagint Bible, the Greek translation of the Hebrew word *hokhmah*, meaning "wisdom". In the **Gnostic** *Pistis Sophia* she is "the Thirteenth Aeon", the divine female emanation who becomes trapped in the material universe. Her penitential songs chart her journey to liberation, culminating in her reunion with Jesus:

... she saw the shining raiment of the Master, enfolding the whole of her Mystery, the Mystery of the Thirteenth Aeon, and sang to the Light on high... and the veils of the Thirteenth Aeon were parted...

SOUTHWARK: London **Borough** on the south bank of the Thames. The old Borough extended a few hundred yards south of London Bridge. Beyond lay open fields and market gardens and, across the marshes, the villages of **Walworth** and **Camberwell**. The delta-shaped settlement gradually spread south, assimilating parts of Peckham and **Dulwich**. In 1997, the London Borough of Southwark was listed the second most deprived borough in England and Wales. In its bid to attract developers to its strip of prime riverfront real estate, the local authority effectively reinvented **Bankside** as a **Heritage Theme Park**. It also secured funding for an ambitious scheme to redevelop the **Elephant and Castle**.

SOUTHWARK CATHEDRAL: One of the oldest buildings in London, to the west of London Bridge. According to legend, it stands on the site of a Temple of **Isis** and the seventh-century convent of **St Mary Overie**. By the ninth century her nuns had been replaced by Augustinian "black priors", though their Priory continued to bear her name. Another legend has it that the first church was built by St Swithin, Bishop of **Winchester** (c. 860 CE). It was rebuilt in 1106 and again after the great fire of 1212. (See **St Thomas' Hospital**.) The parish church of **St Mary Overie** had a chequered history. It was even let to a baker who kept pigs there. A surviving wall, one of the earliest examples of Gothic architecture in London, adjoins the Cathedral's retro-choir. Following the 1539 dissolution of the monasteries, the parishioners were obliged to rent their church, renamed **St Saviour's**, from Henry VIII. In 1614, a group known as "The Bargainers" bought the church from James I. They enjoyed a remarkable degree of autonomy, including the right to appoint their own ministers, which lasted until the 1890s. In 1905 the parish church of St Saviour's also became the Cathedral for the new Anglican diocese of Southwark. The John Harvard chapel commemorates the American philanthropist who was baptised here. The medieval poet John Gower and Launcelot Andrews, the last Bishop of **Winchester** to exercise authority in Southwark, are honoured with elaborate tombs. The epitaph for one Lockyer, a seventeenth-century quack doctor, boasts:

> His PILLS are so well known
> That envy can't confine them under stone
> But they'll survive his dust and not expire
> Till all things else at th'universal fire.

Another classic piece of tombstone doggerel remembers Susanna Barford, a pious, if melancholy, Christian lady:

> This world to her was but a traged play
> She came and saw't dislikt and passd away.

There is also a memorial to those who drowned in the **Marchioness** disaster. The Cathedral's stained-glass windows include depictions of **Chaucer** and his pilgrims setting out from **The Tabard Inn** and characters from **Shakespeare**'s plays. Among the fifteenth-century roof-bosses displayed close to the west door is a wooden effigy of the devil devouring Judas Iscariot.

SOUTHWARK CROWN COURT: On 3 April 1998, the artist Anthony Noel-Kelly was convicted of stealing human remains, including three heads, six arms, 10 legs and feet, three torsos and a brain. Sentencing him to nine months imprisonment, Judge Rivlin told him: "The offence was a revolting one and an affront to every reasonable and decent concept of human behaviour." Under English common law, a body is not "property", since it does not belong to anyone. This landmark ruling established that once "skilled work" (i.e. dissection) had been carried out, the body parts became property and could therefore be stolen. His Honour was at pains to point out he was not passing judgement on Kelly's art: "In this country we pride ourselves on free artistic expression. I sentence you for a very serious theft." The debate continues. (See **Damien**

Hearse.) It would appear that, on the night of Kelly's conviction in Southwark Crown Court, **John Constable** suffered a minor visionary attack in nearby Trinity Church Square. The resulting "Missing **Body Parts**" poem affirms that the Mysteries are not a cult of the dead, but of the living.

SPANISH FLY: (or blister beetle.) Dried and powdered, it is sold as an aphrodisiac.

STEWHOLDER: Brothel-keeper. (See **Ordinances**.)

STEWS: Brothels. The name may derive from the stew- or fish-ponds in Pike Gardens, or from an insulting allusion to the supposed smell of female parts. It could also refer to their function as public bath-houses (*cf.* twentieth century "saunas"). **Burford** argues that Southwark's brothels date back to Roman times, (see **Isis**) and that the 1161 **Ordinances** effectively legalised the "old customs" of the **Liberty**. At the end of the fifteenth century there were 18 licensed brothels on **Bankside**. In 1546 they were suppressed on the orders of Henry VIII, though many, including **The Cardinal's Cap**, had reopened by the reign of Elizabeth I. An engraving (*c.* 1600) depicts 'The Fish Pond House on Stewes Side' as an elegant, prosperous establishment. 'The Barge', 'The Bell', 'The Cock' and 'The Unicorn' all survived into the seventeenth century. The Bankside stews, along with the bear-pits and **theatres**, were closed by the **Puritans**.

STOW, John: (1525–1605). Elizabethan historian, source of the legend of the convent founded by **Mary Overie**. Stow's *Survey of London* includes a reference to the **Crossbones** graveyard.

SUB: Twentieth century S&M slang. One who voluntarily adopts a submissive, as opposed to a **dom**inator, role.

SUPERDRUG: Twentieth-century chain-store specialising in cosmetics and pharmaceutical goods. **Charity**, "the check-out girl", is believed to have worked at the branch in the **Elephant and Castle** shopping mall.

TABARD INN, The: Medieval pilgrims' inn, sited in what is now Talbot Yard, off Borough High Street. (See **Chaucer, Master Geffrey**.)

TALIESIN: The archetypal Celtic bard. Legend has it that **Ceridwen**, the Mother Goddess, prepared a magic cauldron. Whosoever tasted her witch's brew would be blessed with the gift of tongues, and would understand the secret languages of birds and animals. She assigned a boy named Gwion Bach (in some versions, the village idiot) to stir the pot, warning him not to drink from it, on pain of death. A drop of the magic potion splashed onto the boy's finger, scalding him. He sucked his finger and at once heard the birds warning him of the Goddess' wrath. In his flight, he assumed the forms of a hare, a fish and a grain of corn. Ceridwen in turn transformed herself into a hound, an otter, and the hen who pecked and swallowed the corn. She then dreamed herself pregnant with Taliesin, who sprang from her womb singing of how he was older than the world. In the *Mabinogian*, his bardic stanzas show how early Christianity assimilated Celtic paganism:

> And I was with my Lord in a manger in Bethlehem.
> I walked with Moses through the Red Sea of Jordan.
> I walked in the sky with St Mary Magdalene.
> I stole my vision from the cauldron of Ceridwen...
> And I was revealed in the land of the Trinity.
> As I was in the beginning
> So shall I be until Doomsday...
> I shifted shape in the womb of the witch Ceridwen...
> I was once Gwion Bach, but am now Taliesin.

In *The Book of the Magdalene*, the 'Taliesin fragment' embodies Southwark both as physical entity and spiritual state. *Wal* is an Anglo-Saxon word for the ancient Britons (*cf.* Wales, **Walworth**). The man's blue skin identifies him as a Celt. Oak trees were sacred to the druids, and were also used to mark boundaries: Honor Oak is a boundary of the London

Borough of **Southwark**. The "lovely doomed and laughing boy" recalls Adonis, whose premature death was taken as a sign that he was the beloved of the Goddess.

TANNING: The skinning and tanning of hides were among the "unclean" trades practised south of the river. The old Leathermarket and odd street-names such as Skin Market Place are all that remains of the old industries.

TANTRA: Hindu-Buddhist cult, originating in medieval times in the Himalayas. Tantric rites are still performed by naked Sadhus along the pilgrimage trails of Nepal and North India. Contrary to the asceticism of many Buddhist sects, the kaulas or "left- hand" tantrikas practice the eating of meat, the use of mind-altering drugs and magical sexual acts, often performed in graveyards. Tantric sex has nothing to do with procreation, ejaculation or emotional bonding. Yoga, breath and muscular control are used to "open the pathways", to channel the "horny" male energy into its dance with the "orgasmic" female, to consummate the **mudra** of **Siva-Sakti**.

TANTRIC TRIBE, The: In *The Southwark Mysteries*, the Tantric teachings travel west with the **Egyptians**. They take root in the **Liberty**, in the ballads and tales of Bankside **actors** and **whores**. The "tribe" is not defined by blood-ties or even a coherent belief-system. It may be seen as a loose network of kindred spirits, conspiring across space and time to effect certain alterations in the fabric of reality.

TAVERNS: John Taylor, the Water Poet, famously embarked on a Southwark pub-crawl. In his *Travels through more than thirty times twelve signs*, he dedicates a piece of doggerel to the signs of some three-hundred and sixty taverns, including 'The Bear' in Bear Alley:
> No ravenous, savadge, cruel beares are these,
> But gentle, milde, delighting still to please,

> And yet they have a trick to bite all such
> As madly use their company too much.

(See **Ale-houses, Inns.**)

TAYLOR, John: (1580–1653). "The Water Poet". Thames **waterman** and prodigious writer of doggerel. (See **King's Bench, Prisons**.) He was press-ganged into the navy, where by his own account: "seven times at sea I served Eliza queen". Discharged with a gammy leg, he took up residence on **Bankside**, supplementing his earnings as a waterman with verses for births, marriages and deaths. He readily undertook harebrained wagers, such as his bid to row from London to Kent in a paper boat with two fish tied to canes as oars. He would issue advance prospectuses to attract sponsors, as when he announced his intention to walk to Edinburgh with no money in his pocket. Many subscribers to *The Pennyles Pilgrimage* (1618) refused to pay, claiming that he had broken the terms of the wager. He also turned his hand to writing a play, which was performed at The Hope, though it apparently brought him little by way of fortune, fame or personal satisfaction:

> The lustre of all watermen
> To row with skull, or write with pen.
> O had he still kept on the water,
> And never come upon Theàter,
> He might have lived full merrily,
> And not have died so lowsily.
> O twas that foolish scurvie play
> At Hope that took his sence away.

In 1613 he led a delegation of watermen to confront The Globe players at **The Cardinal's Cap**. **The Globe** had burnt down during a performance of *Henry VIII*, and the watermen were alarmed that a plan to rebuild it on the north bank would ruin the ferry trade. The actors were unsympathetic, sarcastically inquiring whether the watermen would like them to relocate St Paul's Cathedral to Bankside. That same year, Taylor was commissioned to stage the first of his many elaborate water pageants. In 1641, he created the pageant that welcomed Charles I on his return from Scotland.

TED: Apocryphal night-watchman in **Britannia House**, healed by Jesus in Guy's Hospital.

THAMES: River, dividing Southwark from the City of London. The old **Borough** is bounded by the sweep of the meandering, tidal river, which has influenced its history since time immemorial. In **Roman** times, the Thames was much wider and shallower; its marshy banks threaded with more than two hundred streams and rivulets. (See **lost rivers**.) The pillars of old **London Bridge** restricted the flow of water, causing the river to periodically freeze over. During the great Frost Fairs of the sixteenth and seventeenth centuries, hawkers set up their booths on the ice. In 1594, John Norden estimated that there were forty thousand people earning a crust from the river-trade, with more than two thousand wherries ferrying people over from the City to Bankside. (See **waterman**.) London's primitive sanitary arrangements were overwhelmed by the population explosion, turning the river into an open sewer. An Act of Parliament in 1847 made the discharge of waste into water-flushed sewers compulsory, which initially only compounded the problem, since the sewers were flushed into the river. One hundred and fifty years later, London could boast one of the cleanest rivers in Europe. A 1990s survey established that ragworms had re-established themselves on the mudflats, a key indicator of a healthy estuarine ecosystem. Seals were sighted upriver near Hungerford Bridge. At night, the city lights were broken by the rip tide to shifting mosaics of pure colour.

THEATRES: In medieval Southwark plays were staged in the yards of coaching **inns**. **Bankside**'s first purpose-built theatres, The Rose (1587), The Swan and **The Globe**, were modelled on the bear-baiting pits that subsidised them. The City Fathers, fearful of the bad influence of **actors**, banned plays within the City walls and regularly petitioned for the closure of the Bankside playhouses. In the mid-seventeenth century the Puritans obliged them. It was 350 years before

Shakespeare's Globe was recreated on Bankside, staging plays by Shakespeare and his contemporaries for an international audience. The excavated foundations of The Rose are in Park Street. Southwark Playhouse, near London Bridge, is dedicated to new work.

THOMAS BECKET: (1118–70). St Thomas the Martyr. Mentor and whoring companion of the young King Henry II. As Archdeacon of Canterbury, he was signatory to the 1161 Royal **Ordinances** relating to the Southwark **stews**. On becoming Archbishop, he renounced his old libertine ways to become the King's staunchest adversary in the struggle between Church and State. When Becket excommunicated the very bishops who had crowned him, Henry demanded to be rid of the "turbulent priest". Four of his barons took him at his word and hastened to murder the Archbishop in his own Cathedral. Seven hundred and three miracles were reported at his shrine in the 10 years following his death. His cult was long established by the time **Chaucer** made his pilgrimage to Canterbury. **St Thomas' Hospital** was originally dedicated to St Thomas the Martyr, but was rededicated during the Reformation, when his cult was suppressed.

THOTH: Egyptian God of science, medicine and writing. He provided **Isis** with the charms that enabled her to raise the penis of the murdered **Osiris** in order to conceive **Horus**. Like the Greek Charon, he ferried the souls of the dead over the water to the underworld. He was also responsible for recording the verdict when the heart of the deceased was weighed on the scales, and for protecting the Eye of Horus. Thoth was credited as the inventor of hieroglyphic writing, and as the author of *The Book of The Dead*. The lost *Book of Thoth* was reputed to contain his magic spells, including the power to understand the language of birds and animals (see **Taliesin**) and to return from the dead. He is depicted as a baboon, or with the head of an ibis.

THREE CRANES YARD: Thameside wharf, so-called because of its timber cranes, facing the site of a cucking-stool where sixteenth-century harlots were ducked in the river. It gave its name to an inn in The Borough. The landlord, John Collett, bequeathed the inn's rents to provide apprentices with tools and to found a school. In 1988 his charity merged with that founded by Elizabeth **Newcomen** to become the Newcomen Collett Foundation.

TOM O' BEDLAM: (or Mad Tom.) The personification of **Bedlam**. He makes his appearance in early seventeenth-century "Bedlamite" ballads. In *Loving Mad Tom* (1927), Robert Graves suggests that **Shakespeare** drew on oral tradition to create the character of Poor Tom in *King Lear*, and that the *Ballad of Tom o' Bedlam* may have been sung at the end of Act II scene iii:

> From the hag and hungry goblin
> That into rags would rend ye,
> The spirit that stands by the naked man
> In the book of moons defend thee...

The ballad celebrates Tom's doomed love for **Mad Maud**, the embodiment of the female mental asylum:

> And I will find Bonny Maud, Merry Mad Maud,
> And seek what e're betides her,
> And I will love beneath or above
> The dirty earth that hides her.

TOOLEY STREET: Branches east from **London Bridge**, running parallel to the river past Tower Bridge, to **Bermondsey**. Local lore has it that the official torturer had his place of business here. Medieval torture was one of the attractions on offer in the **London Dungeon**.

TRAITOR'S GATE: It was an old English custom to exhibit the heads of "traitors" as a warning to others. Vischer's 1616 map shows heads on spikes over the Southwark gate to **London Bridge**, including that of the Earl of Desmond, leader of the Irish rebellion. Other notable "heads" included those of the rebels **Wat** Tyler and **Jack Cade**, and Thomas More, whose daughter, Margaret Roper, persuaded the guard to drop the head into her apron, carried it over London Bridge and buried it at St Dunstan's.

TRINITY CHURCH SQUARE: Georgian square at the south end of Borough High Street. Until the 1820s it was open fields, marked on a 1613 map as "Trinitie land". An 1819 map shows it as "Mr Edward's tenter-ground". Trinity Church (now the Henry Wood Hall) dates from 1824. The following year work on the square commenced under the direction of a builder by the name of William Chadwick. The statue in the grounds of the former church is believed to date back to the fifteenth century and to have originally adorned Westminster Hall.

UNCLEAN SPIRIT, The: One of the Southwark Mystery Plays, in which Jesus drives out evil spirits. **Peter** quotes from the King James Bible (Mark 5: 2–9), spelling out the scriptural source of the "man with an unclean spirit" and the devils who fled into the Gadarene swine. In the case of **John Crow**, the exorcism proves more problematic. Jesus resolves the impasse by adroitly switching to another episode from his healing ministry (Luke 5: 17–26):

> And it came to pass on a certain day, as he was teaching, that there were Pharisees and doctors of the law sitting by, which were come out of every town in Galilee, and Judaea, and Jerusalem: and the power of the Lord was present to heal them. And behold, men brought in a bed a man which was taken with a palsy: and they sought means to bring him in, and to lay him before him. And when they could not find by what way they might bring him in because of the multitude, they went upon the housetop, and let him down through the tiling with his couch into the midst before Jesus. And when he saw their faith he said unto him, Man, thy sins are forgiven thee. And the scribes and the Pharisees began to reason, saying: Who is this which speaketh blasphemies? Who can forgive sins but God alone? But when Jesus perceived their thoughts, he answering said unto them, What reason ye in your hearts? Whether is easier, to say, Thy sins are forgiven thee; or to say, Rise up and walk? But that ye may know that the Son of man hath power upon earth to forgive sins, (he said

unto the sick of the palsy,) I say unto thee, Arise, and take up thy couch, and go into thine house. And immediately he rose up before them, and took up that whereon he lay, and departed to his own house, glorifying God. And they were all amazed, and they glorified God, and were filled with fear, saying, We have seen strange things to day.

UNION STREET: Runs west from Borough High Street, past the site of the old **Crossbones** Graveyard at the junction with **Redcross** Way.

UNSPEAKABLE: The Mysteries affirm that all religious and scientific models of reality are but imperfect attempts to articulate what Wittgenstein calls the "Unspeakable". In the words of **John Crow**'s old **Zen** master:

> word
>> only finger
> point at moon.

VEDAS: Pre-Hindu sacred writings, including the great myths of the *Ramayana* and *Mahabharata.*

WALWORTH: Mentioned in the *Domesday Book* as a tiny manor. The name is thought to derive from Wealawyd or Waleorde, meaning "a farm of the ancient Britons". (See **Taliesin**.) The area had many famous sons: Michael Faraday, the father of electricity, was born in Newington Butts in 1791. Charlie Chaplin's autobiography begins: "I was born on April 16th 1889 at eight o'clock at night in East Lane, Walworth."

WALWORTH ROAD: Busy shopping-street running south from **Elephant and Castle** to **Camberwell**. The Cuming Museum houses a local history collection, including **Roman** artefacts. From 1978 until 1997, the Labour Party headquarters were located here.

WAT,"Tyler": (d. 1381). Having no surname, he was identified by his trade, tiling roofs. Rebel, said by **John Stow** to have started the Peasant's Revolt by killing a poll-tax collector. His Kentish rebels entered Southwark in June 1381. They sacked and burned the **Marshalsea** Prison, freeing the prisoners to swell the ranks of their rag-tag army, and made a point of executing any lawyer they could get their hands on. On 15 June, Richard II convened a meeting at Smithfield, where Wat brazenly presented the rebels' terms, addressing the king as an equal. He demanded an end to the feudal institutions of seigniory and villenage, and "no law but the law of **Winchester**". An argument broke out with the king's outraged supporters and Wat was mortally wounded by Mayor Walworth. His head was cut off and displayed, along with that of his comrade Jack Straw, on a spike over London Bridge. (See **Traitor's Gate**.)

WATERMAN: Old **London Bridge** was controlled by the **City** authorities and frequently became congested. In Elizabethan times, gentlemen in search of forbidden pleasures would pay the Thames ferrymen to row them over to **Bankside**. On the corner of Bear Gardens is a stone ferryman's seat. The waterman's tradition encompasses the legends of **Mary Overie** and Charon, who ferried the souls of the dead over the river Styx.

WEDDERBURN, Robert: (b. 1761). Dissenting preacher, born in Kingston, Jamaica, the son of an African-born house slave. He arrived in England in 1778 and was involved in the **Gordon** Riots. In 1786 he was converted by a Methodist street preacher. Inspired by John Wesley's stance against slavery, Wedderburn himself began preaching in **Lambeth**.

WESTMINSTER: Since the Middle Ages, the seat of temporal power. The Houses of Parliament stand upriver from Southwark on the north bank.

WHORE: Practitioner of "the world's oldest profession". The earliest known references are to the *Kadish-tu*, temple prostitutes, in the ancient city of Ur. The Hebrew prophets bristle with invective against "harlots", although, like Jesus, they tend to use the word figuratively, to denote lust for power and earthly riches in general, and the Roman **Empire** in particular. The poetic conceit reaches its apotheosis in the "Great Whore" of **Revelation**:

> And upon her forehead was a name written, MYSTERY,
> BABYLON THE GREAT, THE MOTHER OF HARLOTS
> AND ABOMINATIONS OF THE EARTH.

Medieval prostitutes with cropped hair were paraded through the streets of London to the accompaniment of "minstrelsy" (*cf.* "our heads were shorn, in carts were drawn" &c). Under the 1161 **Ordinances** relating to the **stews**, the whores of the **Liberty** enjoyed a measure of protection from predatory pimps and stewholders. They were even licensed by the Bishop of Winchester – hence "**Winchester Geese**". The church's attitude was ambivalent. Whores were granted communion, yet buried in unhallowed ground. (See **Crossbones**.) The civil authorities were less indulgent. In 1543, the Mayor "punished many harlots of the stews by ducking them in the Thames on a cucking-stool at **The Three Cranes**". Bored aristocrats would sometimes indulge in a little whore-baiting. The Earl of Surrey and his cronies rowed across the river with catapults to shoot at "the queenes at the Bank". The fate of Bankside's whores was inextricably linked to that of its **actors**, yet they get scant sympathy from hack playwright **Thomas Dekker**. *The Honest Whore* affects a tone of bourgeois outrage, reviving the apocalyptic image of the harlot:

> Your body is like the common shore, that still receives
> All the town's filth. The sin of many men
> Is within you; and thus much I suppose,
> That if all your committers stood in rank,
> They'd make a lane in which your shame might dwell
> And with their spaces reach from hence to hell.

(See **cant**.) To the Puritans, whores were the infernal sisters of witches, and both classes of women were subjected to barbaric trials and torments. Victorian philanthropists set about the rescue of such "fallen women" with evangelical zeal. The issue divided feminists, many of whom saw prostitution as the ultimate depersonalisation and exploitation of women.

A significant minority argued, conversely, that it empowered women to reclaim their sexuality. At the end of the second millennium groups such as Prostitution Pride and **SFC** were campaigning for the reform of Britain's archaic sex laws, which explicitly targeted sex workers.

WHORE GODDESS: "And Her Name is Liberty", whose secret name is OVERIE. **Goose** to **John Crow** and "Mistress Southwark" in whom "the Broken Man shall be made Whole". The **Goddess** enshrined in the hermetic, oral traditions of the **Liberty**, incarnating as a whore to heal the rift between flesh and spirit.

WICCA: Neo-pagan religion, with roots in the pre-Christian worship of the Earth Spirit, often personified as the **Goddess**.

WILKES, John: (1727–97). MP and radical pamphleteer and politician, the "Outlaw" Member of Parliament whose challenge to George III's government made him the hero of the Southwark **mob**.

WILKES AND LIBERTY: Issue No. 45 of John Wilkes' pamphlet, *The North Briton*, featured a scurrilous attack on King George III. Its printer was arrested and put in the **pillory**. Wilkes was prosecuted for libel in the Court of Common Pleas, where he defended the freedom of the press, to the delight of the mob. The so-called "King's Friends" hatched a byzantine plot to discredit him. To amuse fellow members of the **Hell Fire Club**, the MP had privately published and circulated *The Essay on Woman*, his pornographic pastiche of Pope's *Essay On Man*. On 15 November 1763, he found himself on trial in the House of Lords for publishing "a most scandalous, obscene and impious libel, a gross profanation of the Holy Scriptures, and a most wicked and blasphemous attempt to ridicule and vilify the person of our Blessed Saviour." His accuser was the Earl of **Sandwich**, himself a Hell Fire rake, who proceeded to read the poem to a packed House. Their Lordships duly found Wilkes guilty as charged. He was challenged to a duel, wounded, and fled into exile in Paris (1764–68), where he was fêted by the *philosophes* who inspired the French Revolution. In the words of **The Goose**:

> Sez 'e: "I must be off to France
> To start the Revolution, dear."
> Sez I: "Why start one Over There,
> When you can start one Over 'ere?"

On his return to England, Wilkes was arrested and imprisoned in the **King's Bench**, where, The Goose assures us, he lived the life of Riley:

> Here Men Do Time and for their Crimes
> Are serviced by our Industry.
> For when you're in, it's for the night
> To dally with your chosen Whore.
> Yes, Over 'ere we're Doin' Time
> Like it's never been Done before!

(These lines may harbour an obscure reference to the strangest of the **Ordinances** relating to the **stews**, 1161: "Any woman who takes a man's money must lie with him until dawn or pay a fine of six shillings and eight pence."

Burford observes that this provision presumably referred to the last customer of the night. The City Fathers outlawed river-crossings after dark. Stewholders were forbidden to keep boats and Thames watermen were not allowed to moor their craft on the south bank.)

If Wilkes' imprisonment was intended to discredit him, it had entirely the opposite effect. The Southwark **mob** gave him a hero's welcome, escorting him to prison and refusing to disperse. The king's militia opened fire on them: an event immortalised in mob legend as "The Massacre of **St George's Fields**". To the rallying cry of "Wilkes and Liberty", armed gangs swarmed over London Bridge, burning and looting. They even laid siege to King George III in his palace:

> Pell-mell up Pall Mall
> To King in Castle cowering.
> Tongues of flame a' flickering.
> Where the snarling Mob is King.

Wilkes was three times elected MP for Middlesex, and three times prevented from taking his seat. He went on to become the radical Lord Mayor of London, in which capacity he championed the cause of American independence. But, by the late 1770s, he had become part of the establishment. The Goose charts his fall from grace in the eyes of the mob, through to his eventual rapprochement with King George III:

> Sez Wilkes: "What would you have me do?
> But name your price, Your Majesty,
> For I am skint." The King's eyes glint:
> "The price, John Wilkes, is Liberty."

This is a partial, not to say partisan, account. The mob's excesses may well have persuaded him to:

> Turn his coat to slit the throat
> Of his favourite Whore in
> Southwark, betrayed – thus John Wilkes spayed
> The rabid bitch that bore him.

Wilkes himself denied the "turncoat" allegation, retorting: "I never had a coat to turn." In 1780, when the **Gordon** Rioters rampaged through Southwark, torching the **Clink** prison and Catholic churches, he ordered the militia to open fire on them. The Goose's fury at his "betrayal" is somewhat at odds with her rejection of mob rule:

> Now you roast beefs and bully boys
> A-fightin' for our sovereignty,
> I never gave you licence
> To go takin' of my Liberty…
> Then raise your eyes, John Wilkes, John Crow,
> Behold the starry firmament.
> The Works of Man are writ in sand.
> No Work of Man is permanent…

The 'Wilkes fragments' are problematic. They occupy some 13 hand-written pages in **Constable**'s red and black notebook, and were evidently transcribed on the same night as *The Book of The Goose*, yet a mere 10 lines survive in the published poem. The evidence of the notebook suggests that these fragments were recorded some time after 3 a.m. on the night of 23 November 1996, following the transcription of the climactic **Goose's Prophecy**. Thereafter, the muse appears to ramble, exhibiting a singular coarseness, lewdness and profanity. The voice becomes harsh, ragged, untempered by the compassion that permeates the other fragments. The form itself degenerates, its complex rhythms giving way to the doggerel of drinking-songs. One is inclined to think she was indeed "maudlin drunk" when she dictated these verses. And that Wilkes' inordinate place in Southwark's secret history is down to the fact that she was, literally, "his favourite **whore**."

WINCHESTER, Bishop of: The ancient Diocese of Winchester extended from the Thames to the Channel Islands. In the twelfth century the Bishop was granted authority over Southwark's **Liberty of the Clink**. In 1424 the then Bishop of Winchester, Cardinal Beaufort, married his niece Joan to Scotland's King James I in the church of **St Mary Overie**. The wedding feast was held in the Great Hall of **Winchester Palace**. This was the same Beaufort, bastard son of John of Gaunt, who presided over the burning of Joan of Arc. Shakespeare portrays him as a corrupt, worldly man: "Thou that giv'st whores indulgences to sin..." (*Henry VI Part One*).

In *Henry VI Part Two*, Gloucester is murdered at Beaufort's behest. The evil cleric meets a fittingly ignoble end, dying in terror of the hereafter:

Warwick: So bad a death argues a monstrous life.

King: Forbear to judge, for we are sinners all...

Successive bishops exercised their right to license the so-called **Winchester Geese**. Bishop Gardiner is said to have procured whores for King Henry VIII, only to see the Bankside **stews** suppressed by royal decree in 1536. The king's judgement was perhaps impaired by the advanced stages of syphilis. (See **pox-ridden Majesty**.) Launcelot Andrews (d. 1626), the last Bishop of Winchester with responsibility for the Liberty, was, by contrast, a saintly man. He was reputedly a gifted linguist, speaking 18 modern and five ancient languages, of whom it was said: "He would have been a great interpreter at the Tower of Babel." One of his *Preces Privati* (private prayers) is displayed beside his tomb in **Southwark Cathedral**:

Thou, O Lord, art the Helper of the helpless
the Hope of the hopeless, the Saviour of them
who are tossed with the tempests,
the Haven of them who sail; be Thou all to all.

According to legend, the medieval Bishop Peter de Rupibus ("of the rocks") was walking on St Katharine's Hill on the outskirts of Winchester. The hill opened to reveal King Arthur and his knights awaiting their "second coming" at the end of time. Peter asked for a sign to justify his vision to the doubters. Arthur replied: "Whenever you raise your hand in blessing, a butterfly will appear." And so, as they say, it was so.

WINCHESTER GEESE: Popular name for the **whores** licensed by the Bishop of **Winchester** within the medieval **Liberty of the Clink.** (See **Goose**). Pandarus tellingly refers to them at the end of **Shakespeare**'s *Troilus and Cressida*:

> Some two months hence my will shall here be made
> It should be now, but that my fear is this
> Some galled goose of Winchester would hiss.

Being "bitten by the Winchester Geese" was a euphemism for catching a venereal disease.

WINCHESTER PALACE: Ruin, adjacent to **St Mary Overie dock**, to the west of **Southwark Cathedral**. London residence of the Bishop of **Winchester** c.1140–1626. It was destroyed by fire in 1814. The west wall of the Great Hall, with its fourteenth- century Rose Window, survived. A huge stone cross lies exposed in the foundations. Excavations revealed the remains of a second century Roman bath-house. A wall painting, which had evidently fallen facedown when the building was demolished in the fourth century, had lain undisturbed until archaeologists discovered it in 1983. The statue of a British hunter god, found in the foundations of the Cathedral, suggest that the Roman complex included a temple.

WITCHES: In cults of the **Goddess**, "wise women" were revered as priestesses, midwives and healers. As the Christian Church suppressed the female Mysteries, such women came to be vilified as "Whores of Satan". Medieval witches were "tried" by being dunked in the river. If they sank and drowned, they were judged innocent. If they floated, the river was deemed to have rejected them as "impure" and they were burnt at the stake. Charges were frequently levelled against the mentally ill and old women, especially spinsters. (See **Arachne**). Their lurid "confessions", extracted under torture and recorded by the very men who sought to exterminate them, bear little relation to the practice of witchcraft. Such testimony was further distorted by Christian interpretation. The horned god Pan had been venerated as the male generative principle, and Cernunnos as consort of the Goddess, long before Christianity appropriated and assimilated them into its composite **Satan**. The **Puritans** revived the horrors of the witch hunt, making little distinction between witches and whores. By the third millennium **Wicca** had resurfaced as a religion of the Earth Goddess, complimentary to the sky god religions. Some witches used **fly agaric**, **henbane**, **Liberty Cap** and other psychoactive plants to commune with the living energies of the natural world. There were unconfirmed reports that a coven of white witches was operating in Southwark during 1998 to "clear a blocked ley-line" said to be "poisoning" Shakespeare's Globe.

WOODEN O: In *Henry V*, the play which opened **The Globe**, **Shakespeare** evokes the circle of wooden galleries around an open pit (for groundlings):
> Can this cockpit hold
> The vasty fields of France? Or may we cram
> Within this wooden O the very casques
> That did afright the air at Agincourt?

The Goose claims "my Wooden O" as an expression of the spirit of Bankside, where brothels and bear-pits gave birth to Elizabethan theatre. In *The Southwark Mysteries*, the letter **O** is charged with occult (and sexual) significance.

WORMWOOD: In Revelation 8: 11, the "name of the star" that fell from heaven, poisoning the waters of the earth, interpreted by some as a prophecy of nuclear holocaust. (See **Millennium**.)

X-RATED: Classification applied by British censors during the 1960s and 1970s, especially, though not exclusively, to sexually explicit films. In the 1980s it was replaced by the "18" certificate, though the term was still widely used to signify "Adults Only".

YAB YUM: In **Tantra**, consummation of male (**Siva**) and female (**Sakti**) energy in transcendental sexual union.

YAHWEH: The Hebrew name of God that may not be spoken, the sound produced by pronouncing the four letters of the Tetragrammaton. "Jehovah" is a sixteenth-century bastardisation of the word, applied by Christians to their Old Testament God. The early Hebrew scriptures include references to his *asherah* (consort), and *The Song of Songs* was interpreted as their bridal song. Following the exile, shorn of female attributes, Yahweh became **Moses**' "jealous God" of the moral law. The **Gnostics**, tracing his tyranny back to **Adam** and **Eve**, identified him as the false creator god, the demiurge.

YARDS: See **Rents**.

YIN: In Taoism, the female, receptive principle. The watery, orgasmic energy complementing the fiery, horny male Yang.

YORK CYCLE: One of the great medieval cycles of English **Mystery Plays**, staged in the city of York during the feast of **Corpus Christi**. The Cycle comprised some 52 short dramas based on stories from the Bible and Christian legend. Each play, staged on its own pageant wagon, was presented at each of 12 "stations" around the city. The plays commenced at dawn at Micklegate Bar, one of the city gates, continuing late into the night. In *The Southwark Mysteries*, **The Harrowing of Hell** is closely modelled on an original play from the York Cycle.

ZEN: School of Mahayana Buddhism, originating in China, where it was much influenced by Taoist philosophy, and flowering in medieval Japan. Zen uses shock-tactics to transmit a direct, wordless experience of the "No Mind" in the "Here and Now". It deploys *koan*, riddles such as "What is the sound of one hand clapping?" to confound the rational mind's attempts to hold on to itself. "Liberty Zen" is a loose paraphrase of the most uncompromising *koan:*

"If you meet the Buddha on the road, kill him."